Investing in Mutual Funds

NO NONSENSE FINANCIAL GUIDE

Investing in
MUTUAL FUNDS

.

Gerald Warfield

Longmeadow Press

Copyright © 1991 by Longmeadow Press

Published by Longmeadow Press, 201 High Ridge Road, Stamford, CT 06904. All rights reserved. No part of this book may be reproduced or utilized in any form or by any means, electronic or mechanical, including photocopying, recording or by any information storage and retrieval system, without permission in writing from the Publisher.

Cover design by Nancy Sabato
Interior design by Richard Oriolo
ISBN: 0-681-41395-6

Printed in the United States of America
First Edition
0 9 8 7 6 5 4 3

Dedicated to the memory of my grandmother,
Ruth Alexander Warfield

CONTENTS

INTRODUCTION

Are Mutual Funds for You?

The primary advantages of mutual funds are two: expert management and diversification. The miracle of mutual funds is that they can offer those advantages to *all* investors.

For the wealthy that's not so impressive: with a quarter of a million dollars they can walk into the trust department of any bank or up to the desk of any financial advisor and have a portfolio tailor-made to their specifications; they will have enough money for the diversification that prudence requires, and the cost will only be a small percentage of their fortune.

For the less well-to-do, the trust department of the

bank is not open. Financial advisors are available but at a cost that is proportionally much higher. But the most discouraging thing is that even with the advice of experts the ordinary investor won't have enough money to acquire the variety of securities necessary for adequate diversification.

The value of expert guidance is obvious even to the beginning investor, but the value of diversification may not be so readily apparent. Certainly, there's no point in spreading the risk if all your money is riding on the next IBM. But wait a minute: investing doesn't mean finding the stock that will double in a year and quadruple in two. The finest minds in the investment world don't approach investing that way. And neither do the wealthy: They don't want to take a cruise around the world one week and have to sell the house the next. But that's the path you're headed down if you think diversification isn't important. In fact, if you're not convinced that diversification is vital then *this book is for you.*

I hope you're not offended if I assume you don't have half a million. Let's assume you have as little as $250. Well, that's enough to spread your investment over 200 securities or more and enough to hire some of the finest minds in the financial world to watch over your portfolio *very* carefully.

Of course, a mutual fund can't do financial planning for you. There are still a few things you have to make up your own mind about, but they're the kinds of things you've probably already asked yourself, like how careful do you want to be with your money, and what do you want from it: to generate the maximum income, to provide safety in retirement, to grow as much as possible, to provide tax-free income?

Think about your financial goals as you read this book, and you'll see how to achieve them through the use of mutual funds.

$$\boxed{\textbf{O N E}}$$

The Basics

A mutual fund is an investment company. It receives money from many investors and pools it for the purpose of reinvesting in other companies. At any one time a mutual fund may hold from 50 to 200 or more different securities. It may also have a substantial portion of its holdings in cash, usually invested in short-term money-market instruments like CDs, waiting for the right time to be invested.

The performance of a fund is the performance of its portfolio. Some of the securities will disappoint, some will over-achieve, and some will perform within the expectations of the investment managers. The fund's total return, as a result of its diversification, will be resilient against those securities that underperform—and there will always be a few—but it will also water down those securities that performed the best. Nevertheless, this averaging-out process is characteristic of diversification and basic to risk management.

All monies earned by a mutual fund, like dividends, interest, and capital gains, are funneled back to the shareholders. So as to avoid taxes the fund must keep nothing for itself except a small charge to cover expenses, and the securities currently in its portfolio. Otherwise, it could be taxed like a corporation and perhaps even lose its investment company classification.

To some people a company that only invests in other companies may seem a little rarified. It doesn't manufacture a useful product, it doesn't even provide a tangible service except that of middle-man. But since their modest inception in 1924, mutual funds have grown to be the third largest financial industry in the country (after commercial banks and insurance companies). Over 30 million investors have their money in mutual funds.

THE GROWTH OF MUTUAL FUNDS
• • •

In 1990 the total assets of mutual funds exceeded $1 trillion, and the number of funds in existence passed 3,000, up from only 400 in 1970.

Number of Shares Unlimited

All mutual funds have one characteristic in common: they may sell an unlimited number of their shares so long as they stand ready to buy them back on demand. These shares do not trade on security exchanges but are obtained directly from the fund or through brokers marketing the shares. This means that the size of a mutual fund is always changing, increasing and shrinking, according to the number of shares bought and redeemed each day.

Mutual funds are owned by their shareholders, each shareholder owning a percentage of every investment within the fund to the degree of his or her investment. Each shareholder benefits to the same degree from the expert management of the fund and will be paid from the revenues earned by the fund in proportion to his or her investment.

Different Types of Funds

Each fund has its own investment objectives. These might be to earn a high income for its investors, or to maximize capital gains, or to invest only in the medical technology field. The investment objectives of the fund, whatever they are, must be clearly stated in the fund's prospectus, and all investments made by the fund must stay within those stated objectives. If a fund states that it is a common stock fund it will not buy bonds, or if it invests only in U.S. securities it will not buy foreign stocks, or if it invests for income it will not buy speculative shares in the latest pharmaceutical company.

Who Guides the Funds?

A portfolio manager, sometimes with other investment advisors, decides which securities to buy (and when) and which securities to sell (and when) based on extensive research that often goes beyond a purely academic look at a corporation's financial report. Investment advisors go to the companies, visit their facilities, speak with members of their board of directors, and weigh their findings against their knowledge of other companies in the same business sector so as to select the best value for their fund's portfolio.

For the investment advisors more is at stake than a salaried job. Often the portfolio manager is the founder of the fund, and so has a personal stake in the fund's performance. Also, fund managers compete with one another for the best performance. Every year Lipper Analytical Services rates funds based on their total performance for a quarter, a year, five years, and 10 years. Great prestige is attached to the portfolio manager's ability to get his or her fund into the top performance categories.

Picking a Fund or Funds for Yourself

Investors may distinguish among mutual funds in two primary ways: by their record of past performance, and by their investment objectives. Less basic but still important are the services offered by funds and the presence of sales charges or "loads" added to the price of fund shares. In later chapters we will examine how to evaluate mutual funds on the basis of each of these criteria.

CAN A MUTUAL FUND FAIL?
▪▪▪

Very unlikely. Most of the corporations whose securities it holds would have to default or go bankrupt simultaneously. However, a mutual fund can lose money, even if it invests in Government securities, and it can disband, in which case the cash value of its assets would be divided among its shareholders. A fund could also merge with another fund in which case shareholders would receive a proportional amount of shares in the new fund.

The Three Ways You Make Money From Mutual Funds

1. Income Dividends Income dividends, sometimes referred to as "income distributions" or simply "dividends," are periodic payments from the mutual fund. They constitute the passing through to the shareholder of all earnings from the fund's portfolio except long-term capital gains. These earnings may be dividends from common stock, interest from bonds, profits from options and futures transactions, and short-term capital gains such as money from funds temporarily parked in interest-bearing money market instruments (like CDs and Treasury bills).

Income dividends may be paid annually, semi-annually, quarterly, or monthly; it varies from fund to fund. Tax-exempt funds usually pay monthly. The prospectus will tell you when payments are made. You may have the dividends reinvested or a check mailed to you or to your bank.

2. Capital Gains Distribution   Capital gains are the profits made from *selling* securities as opposed to money paid by those securities such as dividends or interest. The capital gains distribution is usually one annual payment made in addition to the income dividend payments. It constitutes the passing through to the shareholder of the net capital gains made by the fund in the selling of securities from its portfolio. Almost invariably the distribution is declared in December. Actual payment may follow by several weeks.

The separation of income dividends from the capital gains distribution is sometimes confusing to investors. Originally capital gains were taxed differently from dividends, but that changed with the Tax Reform Act of 1986 which now taxes dividends and capital gains the same. Nevertheless the payments are kept distinct, and your tax form 1099-DIV will divide your returns into dividends and capital gains. One of the reasons for the distinction being maintained is that shareholders can still offset their taxable capital gains with capital losses on any other securities.

3. Selling Fund Shares   When mutual fund shares are redeemed (sold back to the fund) you may realize a capital gain if the price of the shares has appreciated over what you paid for them. The price at which mutual fund shares are always sold is the net asset value.

Net Asset Value (NAV)

The net asset value, abbreviated NAV, is the market price of the shares, the price at which the fund stands ready to buy back your shares. There may be some charges against the amount you receive from the fund (see chapter 3), but for no-load funds the NAV is precisely the amount you will get per share.

The NAV is calculated at the end of each business day by adding up the fund's total assets, deducting expenses, and then dividing by the total number of shares outstanding. Note that when a distribution is made to the shareholders the NAV drops by precisely the amount of the distribution since that is the amount by which the assets of the fund are reduced. If the distribution is reinvested, then you have in your account more shares so that the total value of your account remains the same. As a consequence, if you want to sell your shares, there is no need to delay in order to receive the next dividend or capital gains distribution. The amount of these payments will be building all along in the net asset value of the shares.

THE NET ASSET VALUE (NAV) FORMULA

$$\text{Net Asset Value Per Share} = \frac{\begin{array}{c}\text{total market} \\ \text{value of all} \\ \text{securities}\end{array} + \begin{array}{c}\text{all} \\ \text{other} \\ \text{assets}\end{array} - \begin{array}{c} \\ \text{total} \\ \text{liabilities}\end{array}}{\text{The Number of Shares Outstanding}}$$

Total Performance or "How Much Money Do I Make?"

The total performance of a mutual fund is a combination of how many and how large the income dividends are, how much the capital gains distribution is and how much change there has been in the net asset value or market price of the shares. Even investors who have owned mutual fund shares a long time get confused trying to determine how their funds are doing, especially if they have their distributions reinvested. In a later chapter we will consider in detail how to evaluate a fund's total performance.

WHEN DO YOU GET YOUR MONEY?
• • •

Income Dividends Many funds pay income dividends quarterly (every three months), like stock dividends. However, a few pay semi-annually or even annually. Almost all funds designed for income pay monthly. The frequency of the payments is stated in the prospectus.

Capital Gains Distribution Most funds declare a single capital gains distribution in December, although a check usually arrives in first two weeks in January.

THREE

Costs, Commissions and Loads

A mutual fund makes money to meet its own operating costs in one or more of the following ways:

1. All funds charge their operating expenses against fund earnings.
2. Some funds add a sales commission, called a "load," to the price of their shares.
3. Some funds add a contingent deferred sales charge if you redeem your shares within a certain time period following your investment.
4. Some funds charge an annual fee, called a 12b–1 fee (or distribution fee), to pay for the marketing of their shares.

5. Rarely there are miscellaneous charges like a "back-end" commission when shares are redeemed, or a commission for reinvesting dividends.

Expenses

A mutual fund is a business much like any other business with overhead, salaries, and the usual operating expenses. It must earn money to meet its obligations, to pay its investment advisors, and to expand and upgrade its facilities. All funds charge these expenses against revenues, that is, they are deducted from the dividends and capital gains earned by the fund's portfolio before any income dividends or capital gains distributions are made to the shareholders. In this way all shareholders pay equally for the operation of the fund.

A fund's expense will vary from year to year, but in general they should not exceed 1.5 percent of the average net asset value for a stock fund and 1.0 percent for an income or bond fund. There are a few exceptions, such as global funds whose costs, because of foreign operations, can climb as high as 2 percent.

No-Load Funds

A sales commission in mutual fund parlance is called a "load." Some funds don't charge a load. They advertise their fund in the media, and they maintain a modest phone staff to take requests for prospectuses. Essentially they wait for clients to call them. The phone staff are not brokers, although they are registered to sell mutual fund shares.

Such funds do not have a sales load charge to pass on to investors. When money is put into one of these funds all of it is invested, nothing is deducted. The fund makes as much money as it can, pays its expenses (which usually run under 1.5 percent), and passes the rest on to its shareholders. Those costs that a no-load fund does incur—such as maintaining a telephone staff and advertising—are charged to expenses which are generally higher than for load funds.

Commissions (Loads)

Some mutual funds engage the services of stockbrokers, financial planners, insurance agents, and others to recommend their shares to potential clients. The advantage of these agents is that they can help an investor analyze his or her financial needs and recommend an appropriate investment.

Usually brokers with major brokerage houses have several "families" of funds on which they receive commissions, so appropriate funds can be recommended. They will rarely recommend outside no-load funds, but most brokerages have at least one in-house no-load fund they can recommend.

A load is expressed as a percentage of the total investment. The maximum is 8.5 percent. Those funds calling themselves "low-load" charge about 3 percent. Usually the load charge is made at the time of purchase and is called a front-end load.

Sometimes a higher risk fund will carry with it a higher commission for the broker. That means the broker has more incentive to sell you a higher risk fund, whether it is appropriate to your investment goals or not.

The Annual 12b–1 Fee

Those funds that do not charge an initial sales commission or load, may instead levy an annual fee of up to 1¼ percent. This fee is called a 12b–1 fee because that's the number of the SEC rule that permits the charge.

The purpose of this fee is to pay for marketing the fund's shares, which may be in the form of commissions to brokers or the costs of various types of advertising. Those funds charging this fee claim that all shareholders benefit through the subsequent growth of the fund. It is true that the larger the transactions of the fund the lower the commissions a fund can get from stockbrokers, yet it is doubtful that these savings are enough to make up for the annual charges. The 12b–1 fee is simply a passing along of marketing charges, every year, to shareholders.

A Contingent Deferred Sales Charge

This is a charge incurred if shares are sold within a specified time period following their purchase. It is stated as a percent of the original purchase price or as a percent of the redemption price. Usually the amount decreases the longer the investment remains with the fund and may disappear altogether after several (usually five) years.

COMMISSIONS ARE DECEIVING
▪ ▪ ▪

Mutual funds state their loads (commissions) as a percent of the total purchase price of the fund shares. The maximum is 8.5 percent, so that if you send a fund $1000, $85 goes toward the commission and $915 is invested. To view this as an 8.5 percent commission is not quite right: $85 is 9.3 percent of the actual amount invested. That's important because your $915 is going to have to grow 9.3 percent before you get back your $1,000. Stated another way, if you wanted to have an opening account of $1000, you would have to send the fund a check for $1,093, not $1,085. By stating the commission as a percent of the total purchase price of the funds shares, the fund make the load seem smaller than it really is.

Back-End Load

This is a load charged when the shares are redeemed instead of when they are bought, not to be confused with a contingent deferred sales charge. The contingent sales charge diminishes over time and may go away altogether. The back-end load is a commission that will always be charged when shares are redeemed. It is rare today, as most funds prefer the contingent sales charge.

Fee for Reinvesting Dividends

Almost no funds currently make this charge. It is simply a commission, usually very small, charged every time your dividends are reinvested.

To Sum Up (Who Charges What)

All mutual funds deduct their expenses from fund revenues before the dividends and capital gains distributions are made. The largest expense is usually the fee for the investment advisors, so there is a direct link between these expenses and the performance of the fund.

For no-load funds those are the only charges. The remainder of the earnings and capital gains are passed on to the shareholders.

All the other fees charged by the rest of the funds are marketing costs that are passed on to the shareholders. They have nothing to do with performance. Funds charging these fees may be more visible because they can afford more advertising, or they may sell more shares because there are brokers or insurance salesmen advising their clients to buy them.

How do no-load funds manage? Generally their expenses are slightly higher than load funds since they charge phone staff and advertising to expenses and not to a load.

How Do the Charges Compare?

...

Let's say you invested $10,000 in three mutual funds: one no-load fund, one that charged a 8.5 percent front-end load, and one that charged an annual 12b–1 fee of 1 percent. How much would each fund earn in 10 years assuming a reinvested annual return of 10 percent after expenses?

The fund with the annual 12b–1 fee of 1 percent is the worst performer with a return of $23,460.

The fund with the 8.5 percent front-end load is not much better with a return of $23,734.

The no-load fund far outstrips the others, returning a total of $25,942.

FOUR

Services from Your Mutual Fund

Services can be a deciding factor in selecting mutual funds, but don't rely on the descriptions of those services in mutual fund advertisements. Check the prospectus for details. Here are samples of the major ones:

Checkwriting

Many funds, particularly money market funds, offer this service at no fee or a low per-check service charge. Minimums usually apply, like $250 or $500, so such a service unfortunately can't replace your bank checking account. There may also be a monthly limit on the number of checks you can write.

If you are in a family of funds and can write checks only on a money market account, you may want to request telephone switching so that you can switch money needed for checking out of other funds and into that account. A statement will be sent to you confirming all checks, and sometimes the canceled checks will be returned. Consult the prospectus for this and other details.

Telephone Exchange

This service allows you to switch all or a part of your investment among the funds within a particular family of funds. You will need to request this service on your application. Several exchanges a year may be permitted without payment of a fee. A statement will always be sent to confirm telephone transactions.

Remember that for tax purposes, exchanges are viewed as sales. This is a difficult point for some to understand, but in order to move money from one fund to another, you must sell your shares in the first and then buy shares in the second. It would be the same thing if you "moved" your money from the stock of one company to the stock of another.

While telephone transfers are convenient and save time, they also increase the risk of misunderstanding because you don't have a paper trail. After the stock market crash in October of 1987 there were major problems among funds verifying telephone instructions. As a result, funds began to record conversations. If your conversation is not recorded, you may want to send a letter confirming a telephone transaction. If you use the "specific identification" method to figure your taxes, you will certainly want copies of confirming letters. (See Chapter 13.)

Wire Transfers

This service is an efficient way to transfer money both in and out of mutual funds. A wire transfer always results in a purchase or redemption of shares, and leaving your account the money can only be wired to a bank. This service must be requested on your application and will require a statement of the bank account number into which you will be wiring the money. A wire transfer may be requested by telephone or by mail. You may want to test the system (sell a few shares and have the proceeds wired to your bank) so that when you need the service for an important transaction there will be no unexpected glitches.

Automatic Reinvestment

When you open your account you can elect to have your dividends and capital gains distributions automatically reinvested. Fractional shares are purchased when the amount of the dividend does not equal a whole number of shares. If you do not need the income, the compounding of automatic reinvestment helps your investment to grow maximally. The majority of shareholders select this option. Check, however, to see if there is commission charged for this service.

Automatic Withdrawal

With certain funds, especially income funds, you can arrange to have checks sent to you monthly or quarterly.

Such payments may be from your dividends or they may be made up of dividends and principal. This option is popular among retirees.

Automatic Investment

Payroll deduction plans can be arranged for regular contributions to most funds. Automatic transfers from your checking account are also possible. Such plans result in dollar cost averaging, one of the most efficient ways to invest in securities. If your actual fund is a load fund, check to determine the percentage load that will be charged.

Retirement Accounts

You may purchase mutual funds in your IRA, your self-employed retirement account, or your salary reduction plan (401–K plans). There will be a section on retirement plans in your prospectus and IRA agreements.

Redemption of Shares

This is not usually thought of as a service of mutual funds, but in fact they make it quite easy for you to withdraw your money. It is the law that funds must redeem all shares presented by shareholders on the day the redemptions are requested (by 3:30 usually), whether by telephone, wire, or check.

On-Line Computer Services

This is a new service only offered by a few funds. Information about your funds (portfolio holdings, net asset value, etc.) and information on your own accounts are available on personal computers through a modem (a device that allows you to transmit and receive data through your telephone). Limited account transactions are also possible, like switching funds.

24-Hour Information Numbers

Through voice-response and touch-tone phones investors can get answers to their questions about account balances, yields, and other information on a 24-hour basis.

What About Closing an Account?

With the exception of money market funds, most mutual funds do not permit you to liquidate your account without written instructions. Check the prospectus as to how to close an account, and if instructions are required in writing then you may speed up the process by having your signature on the redemption letter guaranteed by your local bank. Many market funds usually allow you to close your account by writing "balance" on a redemption check.

Protection Against Fraudulent Use of Services

There is no doubt that some of the services offered by mutual funds offer easy access to accounts. The SEC has begun to investigate the management of these services, and particularly access to accounts by telephone. Some funds protect themselves by taping all calls. Some ask the callers to give an identifying piece of information like their mother's maiden name.

For a discussions of the possibility of fraud on the part of the fund itself see Chapter 12.

WHAT HAPPENS IF SOMEONE PRETENDS TO BE YOU ON THE PHONE?

▪ ▪ ▪

Probably the fund will not be held responsible. Most fund applications include a liability waiver. One fund's prospectus even states that with your automatic telephone exchange feature "you are authorizing exchanges between [XYZ Mutual Funds] by *any person* by telephone."

FIVE

Newspaper Quotations and Total Performance Statistics

The basic newspaper quotation for mutual funds does little more than keep up with the net asset value of a fund's shares. Since a fund's net asset value falls every time you are sent a dividend or a capital gains distribution, the net asset value doesn't really give you the whole picture. For instance, shares you bought a year ago at a net asset value of 10 might have a net asset value today of 9. But if the fund has paid you dividends totaling $3.00 in the meantime that's a 20 percent return on your original investment despite the drop in the NAV.

The basic mutual fund quotation looks like this:

	LAST	CHG.
Kemper Funds		
BlueChp	12.09 +	.15
Calif	7.21 +	.01
DivInco	6.84 +	.05

We see here three of the Kemper funds. To save space, newspapers abbreviate the names of the funds. This should be no problem if you are following quotations of funds you already know—presumably funds you already own or are considering purchasing. In the example above, the first fund name is pretty obvious: the Kemper Blue Chip Fund. The second one looks like a California fund, and thus presumably a tax-free fund for residents of California. In fact, it's the Kemper California Tax-free Income Fund, the dividends from which are exempt from both federal and California state income taxes. The third name is confusing. The "Div" could stand for "dividend," or it could be "diversified." As it turns out, it's the Kemper Diversified Income Fund.

Some names are almost impossible to determine from their abbreviation, like Benham's NITFI fund which stands for Benham National Tax-Free Trust Intermediate-Term Portfolio. In this case the name is even more obscure because in newsprint the capital "I" and the lower-case "l" look exactly alike.

The first column after the name, labeled "Last," shows the closing net asset value stated in dollars. Sometimes it is simply labeled NAV. Newspapers usually quote the previous day's closing prices, so if this were a Tuesday's paper, we would see that the Kemper Blue Chip Fund closed Monday at $12.09.

The "Chg." is the change from the closing NAV of the day before the current quotations. Above we can see that the Kemper Blue Chip Fund closed at +$.15 on Monday so that Friday's close must have been $11.94.

Footnotes for Fund Quotations

The Associated Press is the source for most newspaper mutual fund quotations. Because a simple statement of the closing NAV is misleading on so many counts the AP uses a system of footnotes to qualify the quotations. You needn't try to remember them all, but peruse the following list to get an idea of the kind of qualifications that are important in reporting the daily NAV.

Footnotes for Mutual Fund Quotations (Associated Press)

e ex-capital gains distribution. Shares purchased on this day will not bring with them the annual payment of capital gains paid the day before.*

s Stock dividend or split. An interest dividend or capital gains distribution included some shares as part of the payment or that the shares of the fund split, much like a stock split for common stock. The NAV, and other figures are adjusted for the split. A two-for-one split

---

*Capital gains distribution is usually only once a year in late December. Note that for tax purposes you wouldn't have wanted to purchase the shares the previous day because the distribution would have constituted an immediate return of part of your investment principal, and as such it would be taxable. Because the NAV will decrease by the amount of the distribution, a big minus number in the "change" column on the ex-capital gains day isn't the disaster it looks like at first. It's the normal falling of the NAV after a payment to the shareholders.

For the ex-cash dividend (on next page) everything said above about the capital gains distribution applies. The amount of the NAV will be immediately reduced by the amount of the dividend payment.

would halve the NAV. Stock dividends would also reduce the NAV the same as cash dividends.

x Ex-cash dividend. Purchases of shares on this day will not bring with them the cash dividend paid the day before.*

f Previous day's quotation. Sometimes the quotation isn't current for smaller or less-traded funds.

n or **nl** This is a no-load fund that has no sales charge for the purchase of shares nor does it have a contingent deferred sales load, (a sales charge if you sell your shares within a specified amount of time).

p Fund assets are used to pay for distribution costs. This is the 12b-1 fee, where some charges, like advertising and distribution, and sales commissions to brokers, are paid out of the fund assets.

r Redemption fee or contingent deferred sales load may apply. If you sell your shares within a specified amount of time you may incur charges.

t Charges both a 12b-1 fee and a redemption fee.

More Comprehensive Mutual Fund Quotations

Sometimes two prices are given, a NAV and a "Buy" price (also called an "offer" price). The NAV is always the price at which the fund stands ready to buy your shares back from you. The "buy" price is the price you may buy them *from* the fund.

The difference between the NAV and the "buy" price is the load, the sales charge you must pay to buy the shares. If the "buy" price is the same, or blank, or instead of a price you see an "n" or a "nl," then the fund is no-load fund and there is no charge for the purchase of shares. However, this does not always mean you will not incur charges. Look for a footnote. There may be an annual 12b-1 charge or redemption fees when you cash in your shares. The law permits a fund even with a 12b-1 fee to call itself a no-load fund.

The "change" column, as before, is the difference between the closing NAV and the closing NAV of the previous trading period.

The most comprehensive daily mutual fund quotations are in the *Investor's Daily*. We'll show an example here since enough information is given for the investor to begin to comparison shop for mutual funds.

Rank	1988–1990 Performance Mutual Fund	1991 Total % Chg	Type of Fund	Net Asset Value	Offer Price	N.A.V. Chg
Templeton Group			**Total Assets 9.0 billion**			
A	Foreign	+ 12	w	23.50	25.68	− .18
	Globl Opportunity	+ 25	w	10.37	11.06	− .04
B	Growth	+ 21	w	15.84	17.31	− .01
D	Income	+ 2	w	9.66	10.12	+ .04

First we see that the Templeton Group, the management group, has assets of $9 billion. This figure includes all the funds Templeton manages, 14 in all. Comparing this figure to other management groups, we see that it is a relatively large investment company.

The column on the left gives the *Investor's Daily* performance rank. It is a three-year performance ranking which compares the total returns of all the funds quoted. A + is the top 5 percent; A is the top 10 percent, A − is the top 15 percent, B + is the top 20 percent, and so on. The absence of a ranking, as with the Global Opportunity Fund shown above (the second quote), indicates the fund has not been in existence for the three-year comparison period. These ratings are most meaningful when compared against other funds of the same type (growth, income, global, etc.)

The "1991 Total % Chg" gives the percent increase or decrease in the fund from the beginning of the current year, 1991, to yesterday's close. It is based on the total returns of the fund. Remember, that figure is *not* just the percent change of the net asset value, but also takes into account interest dividends and capital gains distributions.

Investor's Daily categorizes the funds into six types: g = growth, i = income, o = bond, y = balanced, w = international, and s = specialized (as in industry sectors). In the previous quotations we see that all the funds shown were international funds. (Templeton has other funds, not shown in this example.)

"Net Asset Value," "Offer Price," and "NAV" change are the same as in the earlier quotation example. The Offer Price is the NAV plus the maximum sales charge. "NL" is used for no-load funds.

In addition to the basic quotations, every issue highlights four funds ranked A− or above. Additional information given for these funds include a bar graph comparing the fund's total performance to the S&P 500 Index, which is the standard against which mutual funds are measured.

Weekly Quotations

Among the most well-known of the weekly sources for mutual fund quotations are those of the financial paper *Barron's*. A 52-week high and low is given and the date and amount of the latest dividend, but the only bit of additional information that is really useful is the 12-month income dividends and the 12-month capital gains distribution. Added together, these two numbers give you the amount of cash paid out by the fund. However, don't confuse this with the total performance figure (see below), because for that you would also have to add in the difference between the NAV of a year ago and the current NAV. You also can't derive the yield percentage, since that would require calculation from the *average* NAV over the entire year. About all you get, therefore, is an idea of the annual cash flow.

Total Performance Quotations

By far the most useful mutual fund quotations are those that give performance statistics for the last year, the last five years, and the last 10 years. Total performance (also called total return) is made up of the income dividends, the amount of the capital gains distribution, and the increase in net asset value added together and represented as a percent of the initial NAV. Only by taking all these figures into consideration can you get a complete picture of a fund's performance. Such quotations require a lot of information-gathering and appear only periodically in major publications.

For most people, checking total performance statistics is the first concrete step to picking a mutual fund. Financial magazines and newspapers tend to publish one or more special mutual fund issues in which funds are rated according to performance. Among the most well-known are *Barron's* which brings out a mutual fund supplement quarterly. Besides articles on mutual funds, these issues have total return figures for one quarter, for one year, and for five years. In the case of *Barron's* the performance figures are not given as percentages, which tend to be abstract for the average reader, but as dollars and cents. They tell you how much you would have made if you invested $10,000 in the fund for one quarter, for one year, and for five years.

In the second quarter of 1991, the top performer of all mutual funds turned out to be Strategic Investments, a gold fund, which chalked up a whopping return of 34.39 percent. This means that a $10,000 investment at the beginning of the quarter would have grossed $13,439.20 in three months. But gold bounces around from the top to the bottom of the ratings charts. According to Lipper Analytical Services, a $10,000 investment for a year would have grossed $9,983.20, for a loss of $16.80. In other words, if the investor had held shares in the fund for one year, the stellar second quarter's performance would have been completely obliterated. Looking at five years' performance—again according to Lipper—the fund would have grossed $9,646.10, for a loss of $353.90. Such performance would not discourage a "gold bug," but the investor looking for safety and some consistency of return had better keep looking.

The second, third, and fourth funds for that quarter were also gold funds. The fifth in line was Fidelity Select Paper and Forest Products Portfolio, a specialty fund with a 13.94 percent quarterly return. If a specialty fund is not to your liking, we continue down the list to the sixth ranking performer, American Investor's Income, a small bond fund with a 12.76 percent total return. However, checking the five year figures we see a total return on our $10,000 of only $11,519.30. That annualizes to 3 percent a year. Obviously this fund has had its ups and downs. If you wrote for the prospectus, you would find out that it speculates in junk bonds.

The fund that was seventh in total performance for the second quarter of 1991 was Freedom Regional Bank Fund with a 12.56 percent return. Also a specialty fund (financial services), its return for a year was 10.9 percent and for five years an almost even 9 percent. Here at last we have a stable fund with a long-term performance that is reasonable.

The highest-ranking stock fund of the quarter was FAM (Fenimore Asset Management Trust) Value Fund, a growth and income fund with an 11.46 percent return for the quarter. Year return was 21 percent; it was a new fund so it didn't have a five-year performance figure.

Which Funds Do You Choose?

As the above section demonstrates, if you base your fund selection on short-term performance, you could end up in some very inappropriate funds (high-risk, erratic returns, narrowly based, etc.). The technique in using these reports is not to blindly take the best short-term performers, but to choose the best among those that provide maximum safety at the risk level and within the type of funds you are interested.

You should also be aware that the one-quarter and even the one-year performance figures are less reliable than those of longer time periods. Volatile funds, like gold funds, will be at the top of the report one quarter and at the bottom the next. For this reason consider carefully those funds that have performed the best over longer periods of time.

The financial periodicals that have special mutual

fund issues do more than present performance statistics. Ratings and recommendations take into consideration safety, management, price, performance in bear markets, and so forth. Special articles link future performance to analytical indicators like the p-e ratios of stocks in the fund's portfolio (see Chapter 10) or the anticipated growth in specific market sectors. One or more of these issue is invaluable for current data on mutual funds.

"MUTUAL FUND"
ISSUES OF FINANCIAL MAGAZINES

February	*Barron's* (2nd week) quarterly mutual fund report
May	*Barron's* (2nd week) quarterly mutual fund report
June	*Money Maker* annual review of funds
August	*Money's* midyear ranking of mutual funds.
	Barron's (2nd week) quarterly mutual fund report
September	*Forbes* annual mutual fund report
	Personal Investor issue on mutual funds
October	*Changing Times* review of mutual funds
November	*Barron's* (2nd week) quarterly report on mutual funds

The Types of Funds and Their Investment Objectives

Barron's, which receives its mutual fund data from Lipper's Analytical Services, recognizes 27 different types of mutual funds, some grouped according to the instruments the fund acquires, some according to the fund's investment goals, and some according to the industry sector or geographic area within which the fund specializes. To confuse things further, all funds overlap, to varying degrees, two or three, even five or six different categories.

Classifying the funds into major types (despite the inevitable distortions) reduces to a manageable number the funds you might want to consider. For instance, if you are interested only in income funds then you've narrowed the list considerably since income funds constitute only 8 percent of all mutual funds.

For brevity's sake, we'll consider only nine of the most common types of funds. As you read keep in mind that you needn't put all your savings into one fund. You might divide up your nest egg 60 percent into an equity fund and 40 percent in a bond fund. But on the other hand, you could also save the trouble of two accounts by buying a "balanced" fund, since that's about the average ratio of equity to bonds in that type of fund.

In each category top-performing or recommended funds are given. The performance figures reflect total performance, which includes investment dividends, capital gains distributions, and changes in the NAV. Percentages are not annualized unless so stated.

One point: it is difficult to talk about the various types of funds without running into a problem that mutual fund investors often have—understanding the instruments in which a fund invests. Yet it is important to know something about these instruments in order to determine the fund's overall risk and its appropriateness to your investment needs.

So scan the fund types described below, and for those that interest you, check the instruments in which those funds invest. If you come across any (options, bonds, futures, etc.) with which you are unfamiliar, refer to the brief descriptions in Chapter 10.

Balanced Funds

As their name implies, these funds seek to balance several investment objectives: protection of the principal, substantial current income, and an increase of both the principal and income over the long term. The portfolio of these funds is a mix of common stock, preferred stock (special stock with typically high dividend rates) and bonds. Some funds may also trade in stock options and foreign securities.

The performance of these funds tends to be middle-of-the-road since they balance both the risks and return of stocks and bonds. They are on the surface similar to growth and income funds, the major difference being that balanced funds incorporate substantial bond holdings in their portfolio while growth and income funds (see below) favor convertible preferred stocks over bonds.

BALANCED FUNDS: TOP PERFORMERS
▪ ▪ ▪

For the second quarter of 1991 the Plymouth Income and Growth Fund (classified as a balanced fund) showed an increase of 4 percent, and for 12 months an increase of 15.9 percent. Best five-year performance was Phoenix Balanced Fund showing a total gain of 68.5 percent. Prospectuses: Plymouth (800) 522–7297, Phoenix (800) 243–1574

Growth and Income Funds

These funds concentrate on common stock with high paying dividends and preferred stock and bonds that are convertible into the common stock of the underlying company (see Chapter 10). Growth and income funds are among the most stable of funds, combining long-term growth with a steady income. They frequently concentrate in the securities of public utilities, and their dividends tend to be predictable.

Those that concentrate exclusively on stocks are called equity-income funds. If bonds are acquired by this type of fund they will constitute only a minor part of the portfolio.

GROWTH AND INCOME FUNDS: TOP PERFORMERS
▪ ▪ ▪

For the second quarter of 1991 the FAM Value Fund showed an increase of 14.46 percent. For 12 months the Vista Growth and Income Fund increased by 21.34 percent. Prospectuses: FAM (518) 234–4393, Vista (800) 348–4782

Growth Funds

Growth funds invest for maximum long-term growth, and they do so without the use of leverage techniques such as buying on margin. Sometimes, however, they make conservative use of futures or options to hedge the performance of their portfolio. Unlike aggressive growth funds, they usually seek the larger companies which they feel still have growth potential but which may not pay large dividends. The investment advisors attempt to time their purchases according to the business cycle, and thus they are not always fully invested, frequently holding substantial cash positions in money market instruments. A small percentage of your investment in a growth fund can balance an otherwise conservative portfolio and give you the possibility of increased capital gains during a bull market.

GROWTH FUNDS: TOP PERFORMERS
▪ ▪ ▪

At mid-year in 1991 the 12-month total return for Twentieth Century Ultra Investors was 30.07 percent followed closely by Phoenix Multi-Portfolio Capital Appreciation with 27.48 percent. Prospectuses: Twentieth Century (800) 345–2021, Phoenix (800) 243–1574

Aggressive Growth

Funds that fall into this category seek to maximize capital gains. They invest mostly in common stock although not in the larger blue-chip companies that pay the highest dividends. They favor the securities of smaller, less-capitalized companies or companies out of the main stream because of their greater growth potential. Such companies can also, of course, be less stable. Aggressive growth funds tend to stay fully invested at all times rather than holding substantial cash positions as do some of the more cautious funds. Sometimes they concentrate in one or two industry sectors that their investment managers think future economic developments will favor.

Often riskier investment instruments are utilized, like naked options and index futures, and they may also sell short, one of the riskiest investment procedure of all (see Chapter 10). You should read the prospectuses of these funds carefully to determine their specific investment goals and to find out which financial instruments the fund will and will not acquire.

Aggressive growth funds obviously have a high degree of risk. While they often outperform other types of funds in a bull market, they also have the potential to sink farther and faster in a bear market. You might consider these funds for a small percent of your total investment, or a riskier technique would be to switch into them at (what you hope will be) the beginning of a bull market. During a down market it would be safer to abandon these funds and place your money in money market funds or other relatively safe investments.

Do not invest in these funds for income. Their income dividends tend to be low. The major portion of their return is from capital gains.

AGGRESSIVE GROWTH FUNDS: TOP PERFORMERS
▪ ▪ ▪

At mid-year, 1991, the 12-month increase for United New Concepts Fund was 23.75 percent and for Westcore's Midco Growth Fund was 22.25 percent. Both specialize in small, emerging companies. Prospectuses: United (800) 366–5465, Westcore (800) 666–0367

Income Funds

Funds whose investment goals are high income invest either in bonds or in stocks (common and preferred) which pay high dividends or in a combination of both. Sometimes the name of the fund will state that it is a bond fund (like a corporate bond fund), but for others you will have to check the prospectus to see what instruments they buy.

Those funds which specialize in long-term bonds are acquiring bonds with maturities in excess of 10 years. There is slightly more risk to those funds because there is more time for interest rates to rise above the rates paid by those bonds. A rise in interest rates will also affect the net asset value of your shares since the market value of bonds falls when interest rates rise. (See Chapter 10.)

Intermediate-term bonds have maturities from three to five years, and short-term bonds have maturities from one to three years. Funds acquiring the latter will tend to track current interest rates more closely than the other two.

Some investors think that if they are investing solely for income they need only acquire the stock of large companies like utilities which traditionally pay high dividends. But those companies which pay the highest dividends are not necessarily the soundest. In the last few years over 30 utility companies which formerly had high dividend yields cut their dividends or eliminated them altogether. An income mutual fund gives you two hedges against this eventuality: expert investment analysis so that the fund will be less likely to acquire failing stock, and enough diversity to even out the performance of the few under-performers.

There are a wide range of income funds available. Check also under the headings "Bond Funds," "Municipal Bond Funds" and under "Specialty Funds" for Ginnie Mae mutual funds.

INCOME FUNDS: TOP PERFORMERS
▪ ▪ ▪

For the second quarter of 1991 the Eaton Vance Income Fund of Boston (fixed income) showed an increase of 11.55 percent. The Franklin Custom Income Fund increased 6.11 percent. See also the other types of income funds. Prospectuses: Eaton Vance (800) 225–6265, Franklin (800) 342–5236

Bond Funds

Bond funds acquire exclusively debt instruments. There are many kinds, and they specialize in corporate bonds, U.S. Government bonds, government agency bonds, municipal bonds, or foreign bonds. They may also narrow their portfolio to long-term, medium term or short term. All the above categories may be mixed in a single fund, and so it is crucial to determine from the prospectus the fund's investment objectives and limitations. Even those funds that specialize will often hold positions in government bonds. See the section on income funds above for more discussion of bond risk.

High-yield bond funds, a recent phenomenon, invest primarily in junk bonds. Those are bonds rated lower than BBB and which, because of their poor credit rating, pay higher-than-ordinary interest rates. (The point being, a high-risk bond has to pay higher interest rates to attract buyers.) If you decide to take the risk of junk bonds, mutual funds are the safest way (relatively speaking!) to do it. The fund's diversity tends to level out the highest rates on the one hand and the defaults on the other.

It is not advisable to put all your eggs in this basket, but a small portion of your portfolio here could provide a bit of excitement. Certainly these funds are not the place to be during an economic down-turn when defaults and corporate and municipal bankruptcies are the most likely.

Tax-Exempt Funds

Also known as municipal bonds funds, these mutual funds acquire the debt instruments (which is to say, the bonds) of states, municipalities, and their agencies. Interest from these bonds is exempt from federal and from some state and city taxes. Those exempt from state taxes are specific to one state (such as the Vanguard New Jersey Tax Free Insured Fund), and some funds are even narrower, investing in bonds that are exempt from specific city taxes as well as federal and state taxes. An example is the New York triple tax-free funds ("triple" meaning federal, state, and city taxes).

It is important to remember that not *all* income from municipal bond funds is tax-free. Capital gains on the sale of their shares, for instance, is taxable.

Occasionally, legislation is introduced which would revoke the long-standing exemption from federal taxes that municipal bonds have long enjoyed. So far, Congress has resisted taking this step as a means of raising revenue, but as the federal deficit increases, there can be no guarantee that Congress will always stay the course.

Perhaps the biggest threats to the security of muni-

FORBES RECOMMENDS BOND FUNDS
• • •

For the second quarter of 1991 the top-performing bond funds were high-risk or junk bond funds (one of which is mentioned in Chapter 9). *Forbes* in its September issue suggests low-risk "best buys" (of the non-junk variety) on the basis of performance and price. Toll-free numbers are given for prospectus requests. Best long-term bond fund was Federated Income Trust Fund which has an annualized 5-year return of 9.1 percent. (800) 245–2423. Best short-term was Vanguard's Fixed Income—Short-Term Fund which has an annualized 5-year return of 8.3 percent. (800) 662–7447. Best Ginnie Mae fund that was also low-risk was Franklin US Government Securities Fund with an annualized 5-year return of 9.5 percent. (800) 342–5236. Want a junk bond fund? *Forbes* recommends the low-risk Merrill Lynch Corp—High Income "A" Fund with an annualized 5-year return of 8.7 percent. Current yield was 13.9 percent. (800) 637–3863.

cipal bonds are the municipalities themselves. Agencies and cities are increasingly debt burdened, and their ability to meet the obligations of the bonds they have issued has been significantly weakened. While there has been no major wave of city and state bankruptcies, it is not out of the question. Increasingly, the ratings of *Moody's* and *Standard &*

Poor are important in order to evaluate not only the risk of bonds but the risk of the mutual funds that buy them.*

If you are considering a tax-free mutual fund, be sure to check in the prospectus what grade bonds (as rated by *Moody's* and *Standard & Poor*) the fund will acquire. Second, find out if the fund acquires insured bonds. Some municipalities have insurance on the interest payments, and some funds will themselves insure the interest payments on bonds that are not covered. The market value of bonds that are in trouble will, of course, drop, causing a lowering in the share price (NAV) of your fund, but at least there would be some security of the interest payments.

THE MAJOR MUNICIPAL FUND FAMILIES
▪ ▪ ▪

National and state municipal funds are dominated by a few of the largest families of funds, each of which has a wide range of funds covering most states and tax situations. Call any of the following fund families and ask for literature on their national municipal funds and, if your state has an income tax, state funds for your state. Vanguard Financial Center (800) 662–7447, PA only (800) 362–0530: Fidelity Funds (800) 544–8888, MA only (617) 570–7000; Franklin Funds (800) 342–5236, CA only (415) 570–3000; Nuveen Funds (800) 621–7210.

---

*A full treatment of tax-free securities is beyond the scope of this book. To learn more, you can read the No-Nonsense Guide, *Investing in Tax Free Bonds and Mutual Funds*.

International Funds

The internationalization of financial markets is a fact. Modern communication systems, multinational corporations, and new levels of foreign trade have joined the economies of countries to a degree not dreamed of 40 years ago. But interconnected as these markets are, they do not move in tandem. In 1989, the U.S. market was up 30 percent, but the German market was up 50 percent. And in 1990, when the U.S. market was falling, the London market rose more than 11 percent. Another significant example of variance is in p-e ratios, the traditional measure of stock value (see Chapter 8). At the time of this writing, the average U.S. p-e ratio (as measured by the *Dow Industrials*) was 17. In Europe, the overall p-e was only 13.

How to Include Foreign Securities in Your Portfolio

Many brokers advise a 10 percent to 30 percent investment to realize the advantages of foreign diversity. Mutual funds offer two ways to do this. There are funds that invest only abroad, called international funds, and there are funds that invest in the U.S. as well as abroad, called global funds. If you figure that a good foreign exposure is 10 percent, then you might want to put 10 percent of your money in an international fund or invest in a global fund that has about 10 percent foreign exposure in its own portfolio.

What Are the Risks? There are several risks to foreign investments in addition to the risks one normally encounters in domestic securities. Foremost among these is currency fluctuations. Foreign securities are denominated in the currency of their home country, and the value of that currency is continually shifting in relation to the dollar. This means that the normal fluctuations of foreign security prices on their own home markets are compounded by fluctuations in the exchange rate of that country's currency against the dollar.

Market volatility and political instability are, of course, issues in some countries, but even more problematic is obtaining reliable data. Foreign companies do not usually have the same accounting, auditing, and financial reporting requirements as in the U.S. Meaningful information is sometimes hard to get and even harder to interpret. Recently, some foreign companies whose securities trade in the U.S. have adopted U.S. accounting procedures, but for securities in many countries only a specialist could interpret their data meaningfully.

Is It Worth the Risk? Maybe not, if you are acquiring individual stocks and bonds for your own portfolio. Some brokers claim that as much as $200,000 is needed for sufficient diversification into foreign securities. But that's where international mutual funds come in. With a mutual fund you are hiring experts to pick the securities: analysts who are intimately familiar with the particular foreign markets, currency exchange rates, and the financial reporting and political risks of the countries in question. Your investment, even if only a few hundred dollars, can be spread over a large number of foreign stocks and bonds. Even if you use mutual funds for nothing else, 10 percent to 30 percent of your portfolio in an international mutual fund is a sensible way to diversify into foreign securities.

INTERNATIONAL FUNDS:
TWO RECOMMENDATIONS
▪ ▪ ▪

At midyear, 1991, *Money* magazine ranked the G.T. Global Japan Growth Fund as the best 5-year performer with a total return of 168 percent. Using different criteria, *Forbes* recommended the Vanguard Trustee Commingled International Fund that had a 13.5 percent annualized total return over the same 5-year period.

Gold Funds

Gold and precious metal funds run the gamut of speculation from moderately conservative (if held over the long term) to very risky. Mutual funds may acquire bullion and coins, but most of their portfolio is usually in the stocks of domestic and foreign companies which explore, mine, process or deal in gold and other precious metals (and sometimes diamonds). The price of these shares is very volatile, causing fund performance to fall behind and then shoot ahead within a very short amount of time. Gold options and futures and even currency futures are other and more speculative ways for funds to invest in gold.

Check the prospectuses carefully. Sometimes a fund will restrict itself to U.S. mines, sometimes it won't acquire South African shares. Usually the fund stipulates percentages in certain areas like no less than 60 percent in equity securities, or no more than 20 percent in bullion, or 50 percent in companies outside the U.S.

The appeal of gold is as a hedge since it moves contrary to most other types of investments. Traditionally it performs well in times of prolonged and high inflation. If there is a sustained world crisis, gold appreciates: it often rises when all other investments, particularly stocks and bonds, are falling.

Because of its "contrarian" nature, many financial advisors recommend that a small portion (typically 10 percent) of every portfolio be in gold. Gold mutual funds are ideal for this purpose, but be sure to compare the prospectuses of several gold funds to make sure you choose one with investment goals the closest to yours.

TOP PERFORMING PRECIOUS METALS FUNDS
• • •

In the second quarter of 1991, the top four mutual funds in total performance were precious metals funds. Keep in mind that these funds perform erratically from quarter to quarter. *Investor's Daily* gave all four funds its lowest rating. Strategic Investments and Strategic Silver (800) 527–5027; United Services Gold Shares (800) 366–5465; and Van Eck International Investors (800) 221–2220, in NY (212) 687–5200.

Specialty Funds

We include here a wide range of funds with a very narrow focus. Although there is diversity within the market sector that these funds cover, over all they are quite narrow and for this reason tend to be more volatile than ordinary funds. Frequently they will not perform the same as the rest of the market.

GNMA Funds or **Ginnie Mae Funds** These are bond funds that acquire pools of mortgage securities backed by the Government National Mortgage Association (GNMA). Ideal for retirees, they pass along the high interest from home mortgages. Most of these funds pay interest dividends monthly. Ginnie Maes are complicated instruments and their return depends on the actions of the homeowners with mortgages in the pool. During periods of low interest rates, home owners tend to refinance their mortgages; in which case the holder of the original mortgage (GNMA) gets the principal back. This terminates the high interest from that mortgage lowering slightly the interest level for the whole pool. Without going into detail, these hazards are somewhat minimized in the context of a mutual fund.

Index funds A few mutual funds are set up to duplicate the performance of various stock indexes. The performance standard against which most mutual funds measure themselves is the S&P 500 (Standard & Poor's 500 stock index). There is a mutual fund set up to duplicate the S&P 500's performance, and it does so by buying all the securities that make up that index in proportion to that corporation's market value representation in the index. Other index funds duplicate other market indexes both broad and narrow. Vanguard has the S&P 500 fund called the Vanguard Index Trust 500 Portfolio. (800) 662–7447.

Industry Funds and **Geographic Funds** Some funds specialize only in certain industries like medical technology.

Being so narrow, they will be more volatile than the rest of the market and will not necessarily move in tandem with it. Geographic funds include funds that specialize in the securities of one region like the Pacific Basin or one country like Mexico. Needless to say, these funds are for investors who know something about the particular region or industry.

Some funds specialize in certain instruments like option funds or funds that acquire primarily convertible securities.

OBTAINING PERFORMANCE DATA
▪▪▪

All financial periodicals mentioned may be obtained at most news stands. For subscriptions write or call as listed below. Prices are for one-year subscriptions.

Barron's, 200 Burnett Road, Chicopee, MA 01020, $109.00

Forbes, 60 Fifth Avenue, NYC 10011, $52.00

Investor's Daily, 1941 Armacost Ave., Los Angeles, CA 90025, $149.00

Money, P.O. Box 60001, Tampa FL 33660, or (800) 633–9970, $35.95

Personal Investor, Plaza Communications, 18818 Teller Ave., Suite 280, Irvine, CA 92715, $7.87

SEVEN

Money Market Funds

Although money market funds are a type of mutual fund, they are, in fact, a very different kind of investment instrument (and have their own book in the No-Nonsense Guide series). We will consider them only briefly in this chapter.

Money market funds pool the money of investors to spread the risk of investment over many different short-term securities. Investors may purchase an unlimited number of shares, and the funds must stand ready to buy those shares back on demand. But at this point the similarity with mutual funds ends.

One of the most obvious differences is that the share price always remains at one dollar. When you earn interest it is stated in terms of additional shares which are dollar equivalents.

The funds are called "money market" because they purchase only money market instruments. These are short-term debt obligations with maturities of less than one year. There are many instruments a money market fund can purchase, like U.S. Treasury Bills, bank certificates of deposit, commercial paper, and short-term corporate IOUs, and most of these investments are low risk.

Money market funds were one of the first major investment vehicles to offer ordinary investors higher interest rates than passbook savings accounts. At their inception, money poured in from investors anxious to participate in the higher yields they offered. Today there are more than 500 money market funds, and one of the most significant facts is that despite the recent instabilities in the banking industry, insurance, and real estate, money market funds have remained amazingly solid and safe.

Services

Money market funds offer many of the services of mutual funds, but the most frequently used is checkwriting. Shares may conveniently be redeemed by check so that the fund becomes a high-interest checking account. Most funds have a per-check minimum of between $250 and $500. Others have a limit on the number of checks you can write per month.

Many investors spread their money among several funds within the same family of funds and use the "house" money market fund to park money temporarily waiting to be paid out by check or to be reinvested in one or more of the other mutual funds available.

What About Safety?

Money market funds are governed by various regulations just as are mutual funds. They can invest no more than five percent of the fund's taxable assets with any one issuer, and there is a five percent ceiling on the percentage of the portfolio that can go into corporate debt carrying a low debt rating.

MONEY MARKET FUNDS WITH UNLIMITED CHECKING
• • •

One of the most valuable services offered by money market funds is checkwriting privileges. Here are the three top-performing funds that offer unlimited checking. Each averaged better than 7 percent yields at mid-year in 1991. The toll-free numbers are given so you can call for a prospectus:

United Services Treasury Securities (800) 873-8637.

Boston Company Cash Management (800) 225–5267.

Selected Daily Income (800) 553–5533

What happens when the issuers of the debt instruments get into trouble and default or go into bankruptcy?

Due to the diversity of a money market fund, defaults will usually have a small impact on the total yield of the fund. In every case to date, money market funds themselves have absorbed the losses, and the principal of the investors was never in danger.

There is an added safety feature to bank money market deposit accounts: they are insured against default or failure. This insurance tends to lower the yields of bank-based funds, but for the safety conscious investor the cost may be worth it.

Some funds invest only in U.S. securities, specifically U.S. Treasury bills and notes. Obviously, those funds do not need to be insured, but the returns may be slightly lower. Yields from U.S. government funds are exempt from state income taxes in all states but five: Connecticut, Mississippi, North Dakota, Pennsylvania and Tennessee (although Connecticut may be changing soon). Obviously it depends on your level of state income tax as to how much this feature enhances your total return.

Tax-Free Money Market Funds

These are funds that purchase only short-term debt obligations of government agencies below the federal level: states, cities, and their agencies. The low returns from these funds must be interpreted in the light of their federal tax-exempt status. Some funds specialize in the securities of specific states so that they will not only be free of federal income tax, but state and city tax as well.

Quotations

Newspaper quotations for money market funds are simple to read, and unlike mutual fund quotations, they pretty much tell the tale of the fund. Since the share price is always a dollar, little remains to be quoted except the yield. Daily quotations are rare but most papers have weekly quotations. Here's an example:

	7-DAY Yield	WK'S Chg.
XYZ Money Fund	6.35	−.05

The 6.35 is not a dollar amount but a percentage: an annualized yield averaged from the fund's performance over the previous seven days. For the XYZ Money Fund that yield is .05 percent lower than the yield for the previous week, indicated by the -.05 in the Week's Change column.

Some quotations are a bit more elaborate. Here's another example:

52 Weeks High	52 Weeks Low		ASSETS Values ($Mil)	DAYS Avg Mat	AVG. 7-day Yld	AVG. 30-day Yld
7.25	5.11	**XYZ Money Fund**	952	65	6.35	6.43

The 52-week highs and lows are still percentage yields. They are the weekly high and low yields from the previous 52 weeks. From this we can see that the current 7-day yield of 6.35 percent is about in the middle of the weekly yields for the current year. The fourth column shows that the total assets for the fund stand at $952 million.

The "Days Avg Mat" stands for "days of average maturity." It tells us that the average maturity for the securities held by the fund is 65 days. The 7-day yield we have already discussed. The 30-day yield, .08 higher than the 7-day yield, tells us that the current yield is falling.

WANT MORE INFORMATION?
▪ ▪ ▪

The source of most money market fund quotations in newspapers and magazines is The Donoghue Organization, Inc. It publishes a number of reports and newsletters on mutual funds all of which are expensive. However, it publishes the *Donoghue's Money Fund Directory* which gives information about all the major money market funds, their services and past performance. This moderately priced directory is updated every six months and a must for investors shopping for a mutual fund. Write to The Donoghue Organization, Inc., 360 Woodland Street, P.O. Box 540, Holliston, MA 01746, or call (800) 343–5413.

EIGHT

The Prospectus

Throughout these pages you have been urged to refer to the mutual fund prospectus. Newspaper quotations do not give enough information on which to select a fund, and even the performance statistics in mutual fund issues of financial periodicals do not usually detail the goals and investment objectives or the possible risks of a fund. You can obtain prospectuses from most funds simply by calling a toll-free number.

Unfortunately, once having received the prospectuses you've got to read them: each one is 10 to 12 pages long. The task, however, isn't quite as bad as for some investments, like limited partnerships, for which the prospectus can run up to 200 pages of legalese.

The SEC, which governs mutual funds, has adopted a "just the facts" attitude toward fund prospectuses to discourage marketing staffs from being overly creative in their presentations. Glitzy advertisements and graphs have no place here. But for all this bare-breasted honesty the readers must pay a price, and that's to dig out the information themselves. It really isn't so bad as long as you know precisely what you're looking for.

The Date

That sounds kind of simple, but if you've requested prospectuses before it's easy to get the old ones and the new ones mixed up. The date's on the outside cover. Usually they're updated every six months. The SEC requires that they be reissued at least every 14 months. Sometimes there is a "revised" date given, and sometimes the revision is just in the form of an insertion into the document. Check inside for a loose, white sheet containing any updated information.

Single or Multiple-Fund Prospectus

Some families of funds batch all their fund descriptions together into one prospectus. The name of the fund or funds will always appear on the outside cover. If you do have a prospectus with more than one fund, make sure that the descriptions and data you read inside pertain to the right fund.

Loads and Other Transaction Expenses

We will assume at this point that you already know something about the fund since you requested the prospectus. Otherwise you would skip now to the fund description. But even if you know whether it's a load fund or no-load fund, you should check *all* the transaction costs at this point. Those funds charging a 12b-1 fee are allowed to call themselves no-load, which is very deceptive.

No-load funds frequently state on the cover of the prospectus that they are no-load. Even so there can be other charges that exceed many loads. Open the prospectus and the first table you come to, usually on page two, will be the "expenses" table. (If you have more than one fund in the prospectus, it may be on page three or four.) At any rate the title of the table will contain the word "expense" or "expenses," for example:

Summary of Fund Expenses

Annual Fees and Expenses

Expense Information

Fund Expenses

Transaction and Operating Expense Table

Remember, they all have the word "expense" somewhere. This table will be in two parts: Shareholder Transaction Expenses and Fund Operating Expenses.

Shareholder Transaction Expenses This is the listing of all charges to shareholders incurred from the purchase, sale, or exchange of mutual fund shares. The first item is the traditional "load" charge. The maximum it can be is 8.5 percent. Often it is smaller. The second is the load charged when your dividends and capital gains distributions are reinvested into the fund. Usually it is lower than the initial load. The redemption fee is also known as a back-end load and charged when you sell your shares. Exchange fees (if any), always less than initial loads, are charged when an investor switches from one fund to another.

ANNUAL FUND EXPENSES
•••
SHAREHOLDER TRANSACTION EXPENSES

Sales charge or "load" on purchases . . . .None
Sales charge on reinvested dividends . . .None
Redemption fees. . . . . .None
Exchange fees . . . . .None

ANNUAL FUND OPERATING EXPENSES
(stated as % of NAV)

Management fee. 0.60%
Distribution fee ("12b-1") 0.50%
Other expenses
    Transfer agency fee. 0.09%
    Services, registration, postage . . .0.06%
Total Fund Operating Expenses. 1.25%

EXAMPLE OF EFFECT OF FUND EXPENSES

1 Year	3 Years	5 Years	10 Years
$13	$40	$69	$151

The above example is of a no-load fund since no charges are levied in these categories. At one time those were the only possible charges other than the operating expenses of the fund. Now, however, a charge for marketing has crept into the mutual fund fee structure, and it tends to be invisible since it is not shown on the transaction expense list. That is the 12b-1 fee which appears on the next list. Because it is located among the annual expenses of the fund, it tends to appear as a natural part of doing business when in fact it is not. It is marketing charges passed on to the shareholders. The appearance of this fee has prompted some funds—those that charge no transaction fees *and* no 12b-1 fees—to begin calling themselves "100% no-load funds."

Annual Fund Operating Expenses These are the expenses of operating the fund which are deducted every year from revenues earned by the fund before the net asset value is calculated. The management fee is appropriately the highest of these categories. In the example we see a management fee of .55 percent. Most of that will go to the investment advisors who are making the decisions as to what the fund should buy and sell.

The next item, the 12b-1 fee, is marketing costs that are passed on to the shareholders. As mentioned before, these fees go toward advertising, distribution of fund literature, and the commissions paid to brokers, investment advisors, and insurance salespeople to sell fund shares to their clients. Most funds claim that all shareholders benefit from these marketing efforts because larger funds can obtain proportionally smaller transaction fees. In Chapter 3, we saw that an annual 12b-1 fee of 1 percent in 10 years cost the investor more than a 8.5 percent front-end load. In the above table we see that the fee is one-half of a percent.

Under "Other Expenses," the fee to the transfer agency is .09 percent. The transfer agency is the company that keeps track of shareholder accounts. Sometimes this is a branch of the mutual fund company itself, and sometimes this task is handled by an outside agency. The rest of the expenses, listed under "services," are other office and operating expenses. Total operating expenses should never come to more than 1.5 percent, except in the case of funds with normally higher operations cost, the most common exception being foreign equity funds.

Illustration of Total Cost of Fees A short table is given assuming a $1,000 investment, a 5 percent annual return, and redemption at the end of each time period. This table is given in all prospectuses and makes it easier to compare the different fees of funds you are comparing. In our example it is called "Example of Effect of Fund Expenses."

Per Share Data and Ratios

This graph is simpler than it looks. Take a moment to see how it's laid out. Figures representing all the major operations of the fund are given for the last nine years although only three are shown in our example.

Fiscal Year Above the columns with the yearly figures, note the end of the fiscal year. In this case it is June 15.

Net Asset Value (NAV), beginning of the year This is the per-share price on June 16 of each year, since that is the beginning of the fiscal year for this particular fund. Read across the line to see how stable the NAV has been for the last nine years.

Operations All the figures in this section have to do with the earnings and the expenses of the fund from its portfolio.

SELECTED PER SHARE
DATA AND RATIOS

	Year Ending June 15			
	1991	1990	1989	etc.
PER SHARE DATA				
NAV, beginning of year	$8.990	8.478	7.985	etc.
OPERATIONS				
Investment Income	0.470	0.315	0.395	etc.
Expenses	0.079	0.071	0.059	etc.
Net Investment Income	0.391	0.244	0.336	etc.
Net Realized and Unrealized				
Gain (Loss) on Investments	1.544	1.366	1.178	etc.
Total From Operations	1.935	1.610	1.514	etc.
DISTRIBUTIONS				
Net Investment Income	(0.450)	(0.328)	(0.331)	etc.
Net Realized Gain	(0.867)	(0.768)	(0.692)	etc.
Total Distribution	(1.317)	(1.096)	(1.023)	etc.
Net Change in NAV	0.618	0.514	0.491	etc.
NAV at End of Year	9.608	8.990	8.476	etc.

Investment Income Dividends from stock and interest from bonds earned during the fiscal year.

Expenses Fees to the investment advisor, legal fees, fees to the transfer agent, etc. They are detailed in the statement of operations section of the annual report.

Net Investment Income The investment income minus the expenses. This figure will tend to be low for growth funds and high for income funds. As with the NAV, read across the line to see how stable income has been over the years.

Net Realized and Unrealized Gain (Loss) on Investments Capital gains earned by the fund from selling securities in its portfolio constitute the realized capital gains. Unrealized capital gains are the increase or decrease in the market price of securities that are still held in the portfolio, what are called "paper" profits (or losses).

Total From Operations This is how much money the fund has made considering all revenues (actual and on paper) and all expenses but not distribution to the shareholders.

Distributions These are all the payments to the shareholders: the income dividends and the capital gains distributions.

Net Investment Income The total of dividends and interest earned by the fund and passed on to the shareholders, usually called income dividends.

Net Realized Gain This is the capital gains earned by the fund and passed on the shareholder.

Total Distribution The total per-share amount paid to shareholders.

Net Change in NAV The "total from operations" minus the "total distribution." This is the amount that will be added to or subtracted from the net asset value at the beginning of the year.

NAV at End of Year The NAV at the beginning of the year plus or minus the "Net Change of NAV" in the line right above it. Notice that the NAV at the end of one year is the NAV at the beginning of the next.

Financial Ratios

Below the per-share data you will find some sample ratios that will help you evaluate fund operations and strategies.

FINANCIAL RATIOS

	1991	1990	1989	etc.
Ratio of Expenses to Average Net Assets	.75%	.79%	.74%	etc.
Ratio of Net Investment Income to Average Net Assets	4.15%	5.11%	4.36%	etc.
Portfolio Turnover Rate	125%	136%	145%	etc.
Shares Outstanding at End of Year (000 Omitted)	71,413	64,717	59,954	etc.

Ratio of Expenses to Average Net Assets Also called simply the "expense ratio." This ratio gives you an idea of the efficiency of the fund's operations. The average ratio for stock funds is about 1.5 percent and for bond funds about 1 percent. The .75 percent ratio in our example would be good for a bond fund and excellent for a stock fund. Although some international funds have high expense ratios, anything above 2 percent is probably excessive. Keep in mind that expenses come out of your earnings.

Ratio of Net Investment Income to Average Net Assets This is almost the same thing as the dividend yield. Stock funds will have ratios almost half those of bond funds.

Portfolio Turnover Rate The calculations for determining this ratio are complicated and exclude certain short-term and long-term securities. Nevertheless, the ratio gives you an idea of the degree of yearly trading within the portfolio. In our example the trading exceeds the total of the portfolio. Brokerage fees on these transactions are not part of the expense ratio, but they directly impact the net asset value and your earnings.

Shares Outstanding at End of Year This figure tells you the size of the fund and its popularity with investors. A big change in this number from year to year should have an explanation in the fund's annual report.

Description of Fund Objectives and Risk

On the cover of the prospectus a few sentences will often describe the fund, but the complete description will be inside, near the front, and under a variety of titles. You may feel that you are not qualified to judge investment objectives, but don't forget that you are using your own hard-earned money. Don't be talked into an investment you don't understand. If you can't evaluate a fund simply using your own common sense then look elsewhere for another investment.

Funds are usually very careful about the way they represent themselves and their appropriateness to investors. Misrepresentation is a primary avenue for litigation. Usually the objectives of high-risk funds will contain phrases like ". . . of itself the XYZ Fund does not constitute a balanced investment plan. Many of its securities are chosen for their growth potential but they may be also regarded as having substantial risk. . . ." Or perhaps ". . . fund is most appropriate if you are in a financial position to withstand price changes inherent in high risk investing. . . ." You can believe those statements.

Sometimes the description will detail the instruments in which the fund invests. Any that you are not sure about check the descriptions in chapter 10.

Services

Services offered by mutual fund are described in the next chapter.

The Rest of the Prospectus

What you've got in your hands isn't all of it. For simplicity's sake it's referred to as the prospectus, but in fact, it's only the "A" part. The SEC, which regulates mutual funds, has mandated that only the "A" part is required by the investor. The "B" part is sent if the investor requests it.

However, the "B" part mostly makes for disappointing reading. You'll see biographies of the fund directors and managers and how much they each own of the fund. You'll see more details about:

a. the agreement between the investment advisor and the fund, including the expense items charged to the fund.
b. the 12b-1 charges, if any.
c. investment objectives and restrictions.
d. tax consequences of the fund's distributions including the conditions under which withholding for federal income tax will take place.
e. statement of the independent auditors.

Prospectus Updates After you've purchased your shares, you haven't seen the last of the prospectus. By law it must be updated at least every 14 months, and all current shareholders will get one.

Annual and Quarterly Reports

Just like corporations, mutual funds are required to issue annual and bi-annual reports. You'll see graphs and performance data presented in ways not permitted in the prospectuses. Particularly helpful reports include specifics on securities held in the fund's portfolio like their p-e ratios, historical earnings per share, and dividends.

Look for candor in the annual report. A fund that advises on whether the time is right *or wrong* to buy more shares is a good sign. The letter to the shareholders is often written by the portfolio manager and should provide a picture of his or her objectives beyond the rather dry prospectus description.

CALLING FOR PROSPECTUSES?
▪ ▪ ▪

The Investment Company Institute publishes a Mutual Fund Directory that lists over 2,500 funds divided into 22 different categories. Toll-free numbers and regular long-distance numbers are given for requesting prospectuses. Other information includes the minimum investments and fees. Available in book stores or from the Investment Company Institute, 1600 M Street, NW, Suite 600, Washington, DC 20036. (202) 293-7700. Current list price is $18.95.

NINE

How to Pick a Mutual Fund

Deciding on Risk

The amount of risk you can tolerate is basic to all your investment decisions. But how do you arrive at conclusions about risk? How do you know if you're comfortable with 12 percent of your portfolio in high risk securities, or 47 percent?

Because tolerance for risk is so personal, let us consider a very personal approach. Take your nest egg, however much or little, and imagine how you would feel if after you tried your damnedest, your investments failed and you lost half your money. How would you feel? Would you say, "I tried my best and now I'll take what

I have left and begin a new strategy?" Or conversely, would you be unable to sleep? Would you have to alter some important plans for your future? Would you think of yourself as having failed?

OK, let's visualize the same thing, only this time you lose 25 percent of everything. How would you feel? Still bad? Let's try again and say you lost 10 percent, and so on. The point is: *make up your mind as to the amount of risk you can live with by imagining how much you can stand to lose, not by fantasizing how much you might gain.* If losing 5 percent makes your stomach growl, then you are a conservative investor. Choose funds with the least risk. You can still diversify, but not into high risk funds. Can you stand to lose 15 percent? Perhaps you might put a small portion into an aggressive growth fund, and so on.

Implementing Your Investment Objectives

This is one of the places mutual fund investing has it all over portfolio investing. If you were investing in stocks, you would have to evaluate the fundamentals of all the companies you are interested in, compare their price, earnings, dividend, and all the ratios like the p-e ratio and the yield ratio. Hopefully, your broker could supply you with all the information, but the amount of detail you can go into is limitless.

With mutual funds the task is blessedly simpler. In fact, all you really need is the fund prospectus and performance statistics. Past performance, of course, is never a guarantee of future performance, but it *is* something to go on. Volatile funds will likely continue to be volatile; steady funds will likely remain steady, and so on. What you are buying is the chance that their performance will continue within the guidelines stated by the fund.

When evaluating performance statistics make sure you are comparing funds of the same type. An aggressive growth fund compared to a balanced fund will look different and in predictable ways. If you are not sure which funds to compare, check *Investor's Daily* or *Barron's* to determine into which categories your funds are classified.

The Final Steps

After you've decided on several funds you like, weed out the new funds. They don't have enough of a track record to evaluate, and besides, new funds often have startup problems. Why take on the extra risk? Stick to funds that have been around three years or more.

Second, take out the smallest funds. Small funds can have high cost in proportion to their assets.

Third, take a hard look at the fund's past performance. If it fell by 10 percent or more in any given year, then look for a good reason or avoid that fund altogether. A conservative investor should stay away from any fund that has lost more than 5 percent in any given year (from the previous year) and never touch one that has posted an annual loss.

Fourth, compare the investment strategy as stated in the prospectus. Is it the way you would invest? The statement should be clear and make sense. The prospectus is not for industry professionals, it's for investors like you. If you don't understand what you read, don't buy. If you don't like what you read, don't invest, no matter how highly the fund is recommended.

How Many Funds Should You Have?

If you have under $5,000 to invest and are not retired, you should consider a single low-risk fund such as a balanced fund where you have the potential for capital gains through stock holdings and income through bonds. These types of funds are stable, which means they will not be the leaders in a bull market, but they also will not fall as far as some others in a bear market. At your stage of investment you would not want the risk of more specialized funds.

If you have over $5,000 to invest, you may want to consider holding more than one fund. Because mutual funds already represent diversity and reduced risk, the purpose of diversity is not the same as for a stock portfolio. For instance, in a stock portfolio you might acquire the shares of five or six utility companies, but you would hardly need five or six income-type mutual funds. That would add to your bookkeeping and perhaps even to your expenses. You could even be in the peculiar position of holding a fund that is acquiring a security while another is selling it.

The purpose of diversity in a mutual fund portfolio is to shape the portfolio according to your needs and investment goals. Ask yourself what your over-all goals are, what your time frame is, and how much appetite you have for risk. The answers to these questions will help you in the selection of the fund categories in which you want to invest.

Some financial advisors, in order to spread the focus of a mutual fund portfolio over several areas, recommend up to 10 different funds, but even with only a single investment focus some diversity is appropriate. For instance, those interested solely in income might split their money between a corporate bond fund, a government bond fund, and a utility fund.

HOW DO YOU MANAGE A GROUP OF MUTUAL FUNDS?

• • •

If you have more than three or four mutual funds, you may want to open an account with a discount stockbroker. There are several that allow you to buy and hold hundreds of different mutual funds in your account. There will be small transaction fees from the brokerage, so no-load funds are the most appropriate to be held this way. Your statements will show all of your mutual funds together: purchase prices, dividends, sales, NAVs, etc.

Other Types of Performance Ratings

One of the problems of performance statistics is that they are no guarantee of future performance, as the warning on every prospectus reads. However, a recent study (Roger Ibbotson, Yale University and William Goetzman, Columbia University) has concluded that funds with good past performance have a 60 percent chance of repeating that performance, so apparently, past performance statistics are at least *some* reason to chose a fund.

Nevertheless, don't overlook various other ways of rating fund performance. The p-e ratio is one of those ways. (See chapter 10 for a discussion of p-e ratio.) The average of the p-e ratios of a fund's portfolio is a window on a fund's investment strategy. Value oriented funds will typically have a low p-e ratio, acquiring high-dividend utility companies. Current income and not growth is their emphasis. Growth funds, on the other hand, will sport high p-e ratios.

High and low are, of course, relative terms. In the second quarter of 1991, the average p-e for the Dow Jones Industrial Average was 16.8. The fund with the lowest p-e during the second quarter of 1991 was Stratton Monthly Dividend, classified as a utilities fund, with a p-e of 11.5, well below the DJIA average. The p-e's of growth funds, on the other hand, soared into the 30s and 40s. If one decided to opt for the lowest p-e in the growth fund category, that would go to the Bruce Fund, with a p-e of 12.3. This in contrast to the highest growth fund, which had a p-e of 43.2.

AN INEXPENSIVE MUTUAL FUND NEWSLETTER
•••

The *Mutual Fund Forecaster* is just for mutual funds and contains performance statistics, projections, and articles with best-buy recommendations. Write Institute for Economic Research, 3471 North Federal Highway, Ft. Lauderdale, FL 33306 or call (800) 327–6720. Cost is $45 per year with a 6-month money back trial subscription.

TEN

The Investments a Mutual Fund Buys

A detailed knowledge of stocks, bonds, options, and money market instruments is not necessary for the investor in mutual funds, but it is helpful to know the major characteristics of the instruments in which a mutual fund invests, because recommendations and comparisons of and between funds often hinge on discussions of these instruments. For example, an income fund might claim as one of its objectives the purchase of stocks with a low p-e ratio. Does that sound like a good idea to you? And what about a growth fund that states in its prospectus that it will write covered options? Should you run the other way?

Our excursion into these instruments will be brief,

and in every case the relationship to mutual funds made clear.

Common Stock

Common stocks (also called shares) are a unit of ownership in a corporation. In fact, corporations cannot be owned any other way than through their shares. Because they constitute ownership, stocks are referred to as equity instruments.

As owners of a corporation, stockholders share in the fortune of their corporation in two ways: through capital gains and through dividends. If the company prospers and the market price of the share rises, shareholders may sell these shares at a profit, thus realizing capital gains. If the company makes a profit, the board of directors may decide to distribute some of that profit to the shareholders by means of dividends.

Shareholders of a mutual fund are not considered equity owners of the corporations in which the fund holds stock. The fund is considered the owner, and the fund may vote its shares as it chooses. Individuals seldom hold enough shares in a corporation to make a real difference in corporate votes, but mutual funds may own thousands of shares and as such be a substantial voice on shareholder issues.

P-E Ratio of Common Stocks

One of the measures of value of common stock is the p-e ratio. Mutual funds will often quote the p-e ratio of the stocks they hold to demonstrate a conservative low-risk approach or an aggressive greater-risk approach to their fund's performance.

P-e ratio stands for price-earnings ratio. Briefly, it's the number of times the price exceeds the per-share earnings. If a company makes a million dollars in profit and it has a million shares outstanding, then its earnings per share is $1. If the market price for that security is $10, then the per-share price is 10 times the per-share earnings. The p-e ratio would be 10.

Conservative, established companies usually have lower p-e ratios like 5 or 15. Growth companies can have higher ratios like 20 to 30. Purchasing shares with low p-e ratios is thought of as purchasing value. Certainly you are purchasing more earning power. Some industries, like utilities, have traditionally low p-e ratios. Some have traditionally high p-e ratios, like pharmaceutical companies. The comparison of p-e ratios is most meaningful between companies in the same industry sector.

Stock Prices and the Net Asset Value

The market price of stocks is a complex of many things: fundamentals like the p-e ratio, assets, dividends, investor expectation, and downright emotion. This contrasts sharply with the Net Asset Value. The net asset value is a precise number arrived at by dividing up the assets (the market value of the securities held) and dividing by the number of shares outstanding. There is no raising or lowering the NAV because of demand or investor confidence or hysteria. The net asset value is the value of the shares and that's what you'll get if you sell them back to the fund.

Preferred Stock

Preferred stock is closer to bonds than to stock. It doesn't represent equity in a company and pays a high dividend stated as a percent of the face value, like a bond. But preferred shares don't mature like bonds. They are usually purchased for their high dividend, and mutual funds seeking high income invest heavily in them. Sometimes preferred shares can be converted into common shares of the underlying common stock. See "convertible securities" later in this chapter.

Bonds

Bonds are loans. In contrast to stocks, which are equity instruments, bonds are debt instruments. Bonds are usually denominated at $1,000, which is called their face value. They pay a fixed interest (the "coupon rate"), and they return the face value of the bond to the bond holder at maturity. When a mutual fund says in its prospectus that it invests in fixed-income securities, it means bonds (and sometimes certificates of deposit with a maturity of longer than one year).

There are generally three types of bonds: corporate bonds, municipal bonds, and government bonds. Independent rating companies like *Standard & Poor* and *Moody's* rate bond issues according to the financial shape of the issuing company and its ability to make interest payments and return the interest at maturity. Bonds with a low rating must pay high rates of interest to attract buyers and are considered riskier investments. High rated bonds pay less interest but are considered far more reliable investments. Mutual funds which invest in bonds state the investment grade bonds in which they invest. *Be sure to check this in any bond fund prospectus you receive.* Those funds which buy bonds with higher yields are taking on a much higher degree of risk. In general, the bond funds that are the safest pay the lowest interest rates.

The price of bonds is affected by interest rates. Let's say you own a bond for which you paid $1,000 and which pays 5 percent interest. The fixed interest amount is also called the coupon rate. The bond will pay $50 a year, which is 5 percent of the face value. If the prevailing interest rate for bonds of the same quality is 7 percent, then you will have to come down on your price to sell the bond. Why would anyone pay you $1,000 for your bond paying 5 percent when they could buy one for the same price that pays 7 percent? When you lower the price of your bond, say to $712, then the $50 yearly interest return will be just a bit above 7 percent. By adjusting the price of the bond, you bring its yield in line with current interest rates. That's why bonds are so sensitive to interest rates.

Some people have the mistaken idea that longer-term bonds are less risky than short term bonds. After all, the yield return is set for a longer period of time. But in fact, longer-term bonds are considered more risky. Those people who bought the long-term U.S. government bonds with a 4 percent coupon rate might have done so when the prevailing rates were around 4 percent. The risk they took was that within the 20 or 30 years of the bond's life, interest rates might rise above the coupon rate of their bond and render their return far less attractive than it was when they bought it. Sure enough, that's what happened.

As a result, the price of long-term bonds is more volatile than for medium or short-term bonds. If interest rates rise 1 percent, the price of long-term bonds is likely to fall an even greater percent. The reason is that the bond has so many years left paying what is now a low interest rate.

Yield to maturity is an important concept in the bond world. It is an attempt to evaluate the return of a bond by taking into consideration the fact that the face value is returned at maturity.

Let's say you sold that bond we talked about before for $712 so that its $50 yearly interest rate would yield about 7 percent for the new purchaser. But what if that bond had only a year left to maturity? At the end of the year the bond issuer will have paid the $50 one-year interest, and then it will pay the bond holder the face value of the bond, $1,000. That's $287 profit (capital gain) in addition to the interest. Obviously this fact should affect the selling price of the bond. You wouldn't dream of selling it for $712. $980 would be more like it, to balance out the capital gain.

The mechanism for pricing bonds is complex and completely different from stocks. It depends to a great deal on the rating of the bond and the current interest rates (in conjunction with the coupon rate) and the maturity date. For this reason, as a debt instrument bonds are safer than stocks, because interest payments take precedence over the payment of dividends. In case of dissolution, the bondholders have prior claim to the assets of the company. After all, the bills must be paid first, then the owners get what's left.

A mutual fund that invests in bonds is emphasizing current income and de-emphasizing future capital gains.

Ginnie Mae Mutual Funds

Ginnie Maes are not easy to understand. The Government National Mortgage Association (GNMA) buys mortgages backed by the FHA and the VA. They create pools of these mortgages and issue bonds on them. As usual with real estate mortgages, home owners pay off both interest and principal in their payments. Both principal and interest are passed through the GNMA and on to the bond holders. In the case of mutual funds that invest in these bonds, the money eventually passes on to the fund shareholders.

Such funds are for people who want maximum current income, like retirees. Some people think these mortgages are backed by the U.S. government. They are not, but they *are* backed by an agency of the U.S. government.

The problem with Ginnie Maes is that during periods of low interest rates, home owners tend to refinance their mortgages. As the pool of mortgages dries up, much of the principal is returned through the pool and on to the investors who don't want their principal back—they want high interest. Most home mortgages are for 30 years but because of refinancing, the average payback is only 12 years.

What this does is cause the yield on Ginnie Maes to fall during periods of low interest rates. Investors mustn't think they have locked in any particular rate of return when they buy a Ginnie Mae fund. Mutual funds do tend to even out a lot of unreliable performance, but it is unavoidable that yields will fall during periods of low interest rates. Even so, the rates are among the highest available to investors looking for current income.

Convertible Securities

Frequently you see in mutual fund prospectuses that the fund invests in convertible securities. Convertibility is a feature of some preferred stocks and some bonds. What it means is that the preferred stock or bond with a convertible feature can be converted, under certain terms, into the common stock of the underlying company.

Preferred stocks and bonds yield more than common stock, so they are good for income. On the other hand, they can be converted into stock so that capital appreciation is also possible. A bond that can be converted into 100 shares of XYZ will be worth far more than its face value ($1,000) if the shares of XYZ are at $15. In this case, the price of the bond would tend to track, at a different level, the market price of the stock. The same for preferred shares. The mutual fund would have to decide whether the higher yielding preferred shares or bonds should be held or capital gains should be taken in selling the security or converting it into the underlying shares of common stock.

Money Market Instruments

Every fund has to keep some cash in the short term, and so money market instruments are used to keep its cash producing while waiting to be paid out or reinvested. Money market instruments have maturities of less than one year. The major categories are U.S. Treasury bills, certificates of deposit, and commercial paper. All are debt instruments, of the U.S. government or of banks and corporations.

Options

Options are contracts to buy or sell stocks, bonds, or futures. The holder of an option does not own the underlying securities, but merely the right to buy or to sell them at a certain price.

Options are not available on all securities, only on those of certain larger companies. The way they work is complicated but basically, if an option you bought gave you the right to buy 100 shares of XYZ stock at $12.00 a share and those shares were selling on the stock market for $10.00 a share, the option wouldn't be worth much. But what if the option were good for three months, and what if two months later XYZ was selling at $15.00 per share? An option for 100 shares would be worth at least $300, maybe more if the price of XYZ continued to rise.

The option described above is a call option, allowing you to purchase shares. You can either buy or sell a call. Options allowing you to sell a security are called puts, and you can buy or sell puts, too. The combinations are many and imaginative. They are much more speculative than stocks or bonds because they represent neither equity or debt.

There is a technique called "writing covered options" that involves selling options on stocks you own. It is a relatively conservative strategy that assures the owner of the stock a guaranteed return. The writers of covered options never get into deep trouble since the worst that can happen is that they don't make quite as much money on a stock whose price increases as they otherwise might. Here's how it works:

An investor owns 100 shares in XYZ which is selling for $10 per share. The investor, instead of buying a call option, *sells* a call option giving someone else the right to buy XYZ from him at $12 per share. Why would an investor do this? For extra money. The investor has the dividend from the stock and also receives a price for the sale of the call option.

The standard options are for nine months. If in this time the price of XYZ doesn't rise above $12, no investor in his right mind would exercise the option. Why would he want to buy the shares from you at $12 when he could buy them on the open market for less? At the end of the nine months the seller of the option, called the "writer" in option terminology, still has the stock, the money from the sale of the option, and the option expires.

If the price of XYZ *does* rise above $12, then the investor is not in serious trouble. An option can be canceled (called closing the position) by buying the opposite one, so you would cancel the sale of a call by buying a call with the same terms. This will probably wipe out the money you made on the sale of the option and possibly more. If the option is exercised—that is, if someone holding the option you sold demands to buy the shares—you lose the shares but you still get $12 per share, more than they were worth when you sold the option.

A risky use of options is when you sell options on

securities you don't own. Those are called "naked" options and are far more speculative.

What if your mutual fund deals in options? If the prospectus specifically states the fund sells covered options then it is a relatively conservative technique. If it simply says the fund may write or sell options, then it gives itself the latitude to deal in naked options. If you are in an aggressive fund that deals in naked options, then you should know that you are exposing yourself to real risk. Read the prospectus carefully and don't invest unless you understand and agree with the strategies of the portfolio manager.

Futures

Futures contracts are a lot like the options described above, except they deal in commodities or financial instruments instead of stock. Only the more aggressive funds will trade in futures.

One particularly important type of future is one of the newest on the financial scene: the Index future. Basically it is a contract to buy or sell a basket of securities that matches a stock index. These futures might be used to bring the fund more closely in line with the returns of the index they are based on.

Don't assume that Index Mutual Funds all deal in futures. Some may try to duplicate the results of a particular index by investing in the actual securities of that index.

ETHICS OF A MUTUAL FUND'S INVESTMENTS

▪ ▪ ▪

Are you concerned about the ethics of investing? The monthly magazine, *Investing for a Better World,* rated corporations on the basis of environmental issues, employee relations, and community involvement. No companies involved in alcohol, animal testing, gambling, nuclear power, South Africa, tobacco or weapons were considered. The five best-performing mutual funds which invested along ethical lines are listed below with last-year's total returns and phone numbers. Pas World (22.4 percent) 800 767–1729, Progressive Environmental (22.4 percent) 800 826–8154, Calvert-Ariel Appreciation (21.6 percent) 800 368–2748, Dreyfus Third Century (21.5 percent) 800 645–6561, and Parnassus (17.3 percent) 800 999–3505. *Investing for a Better World* is $19.95 per year. Call 617–423–6655.

ELEVEN

When to Sell

A great deal of attention has been given to selecting a mutual fund, but what about selling one? Are there danger signals that should tell the prudent investor when to bail out? The criteria mentioned below are the kinds of cautions you will encounter in advisory letters or financial periodicals that review mutual funds. Even if you feel you are not in a position to evaluate a fund first hand, this discussion will help you interpret the recommendations of others.

Poor Performance

Funds are bought for their promise of performance. If they don't live up to expectation, do you sell after six months, a year, two? Some advisors claim that you need to evaluate a fund's performance over a full market cycle, which is typically four or five years. But it's better to do that kind of evaluation on *past* performance before you buy into a fund and not with a fund whose shares you are sitting on for all that time. If a fund underperforms other funds *of its type*, a year is long enough. Get rid of it.

What constitutes poor performance? The secret to evaluating a fund's performance is to compare it with the performance of similar funds. An aggressive growth fund with an annual total performance of 8 percent is poor when its peers turn up 12 percent and 13 percent. A performance of 2 percent is good if the other funds of that the same type all lose money. When the market sector covered by your particular fund is in a general decline, then all the funds covering that sector will decline, too. For narrowly based funds that may only mean that that particular kind or area of investment is out of fashion. Poor performance alone is not enough, it has to be poor performance in relation to other funds of a similar type.

You also might compare your fund's performance with market indexes. If you hold a utility fund, compare it with the Dow Jones Utility Average: an index much like the Dow Jones Industrial Average which can be found in most newspapers. Growth funds and growth-and-income funds can be compared to the Standard & Poor's 500 index, a standard for the whole mutual fund community. A fund that specializes in small companies could be compared to the NASDAQ Composite index, again, found in most newspapers.

A Change of Managers

The fund's investment advisors, particularly the portfolio manager, must take the credit or blame for the fund's total return, and the news of the portfolio manager's departure may or may not be a sign of change in performance. Whoever inherits the fund inherits the entire portfolio, and it will take time for the effect of the new management to be felt. Nevertheless, after the loss of a manager you should watch a fund's performance more often than quarterly.

Some funds emphasize a team approach. They claim it guarantees continuity in case someone leaves. That depends on whether you believe the senior advisor really doesn't run the show. Certainly that approach guarantees that fewer investors will be upset at the loss of any one individual.

High Expense Ratio

As a shareholder you will periodically receive updated prospectuses. Be sure to check each time the yearly expense ratio. It will be quoted as a percent of the average net asset value under the per-share data (see chapter 8). If it has climbed for several years, that is a possible sell signal. Check also to see if a 12b-1 fee has been imposed. That won't affect the expense ratio but it will impact negatively on the net asset value. Check the number of shares outstanding. If the fund has shrunk then transaction fees could be eating up a higher percentage of profits. Also, increased turnover could be the culprit.

Whatever level the expenses, keep in mind that they should not, under ordinary circumstances, go above 1.5 percent. About the only exception is international funds where the cost of transactions in foreign countries can raise the expense ratio as high as 2 percent.

Inconsistent Investments

A fund states its investment objectives in its prospectus. No security in its portfolio should be an exception. It is unlikely that a fund's advisors would purchase a security outside the fund's stated goals but what about a security already in its portfolio? For example, if a bond fund retains bonds after their ratings have dropped, it could be holding securities below the safety level states in the prospectus. There might be a reluctance to liquidate such bonds because there would likely be a capital loss. (Such bonds would be worth less.) But the net effect of retaining those bonds is an increase in the risk level of the fund. You should consider selling such a fund.

WANT THE FACTS?

• • •

The Investment Company Institute publishes the *Mutual Fund Fact Book*. Updated every year, this little book contains a wealth of information and statistics about the mutual fund industry. It does not contain information on specific funds but is instead "a basic guide to the trends and statistics that were observed and recorded during the year." Write Michelle Worthy, Investment Company Institute, 1600 M Street, NW, Suite 600, Washington, DC 20036. The price is $15.00.

TWELVE

The Chances of Fraud

Mutual fund investors are safer from loss resulting from fraud on the part of management than are most other investors. Why? Because the transfer of profit and risk to the shareholders makes for little incentive to indulge in illegal activities. That's not to say that mutual fund shareholders don't lose money, or that there is never fraud, but this simple principle of mutual fund structure is the next-best thing as a guarantee that investor losses will seldom be from illegal activities.

In a general market decline, those funds which are diversified across the general market also decline. That's part of the short-term risk of securities investments. Likewise, when fund managers make poor choices their funds underperform other funds within the same category. The point is that the risk, of both a market downturn and of poor management, has been transferred to the fundholders. The fund managers do not lose money—although they might eventually lose their jobs.

More to the point with respect to fraud, the profit of the fund is transferred to investors. Therefore, why would a fund manager indulge in any shady dealings only for the fruits of his labor to be passed on to others? Scandals on Wall Street involve bankers and brokers breaking the law for their own aggrandizement. A fund manager, working for a tiny percentage of the revenues, normally has insufficient incentive to take on the risk of breaking the law.

Checks and Balances

Mutual funds are regulated by the Investment Company Act of 1940. There are several important checks built into their structure which discourage any illegal goings-on. First of all, the assets of the fund are not held by the fund's investment advisors. They are held in safekeeping by an independent third party, called a custodian, which is usually a bank. The custodian's job it is to record all fund investment transactions, account for all assets, and safekeep all securities. It would be difficult for an unscrupulous investment advisor to conceal assets or transfer them to illegal accounts without those activities being noticed right away or at the very least leaving a paper trail.

The difficulties recently experienced in other financial sectors have arisen sometimes because problems were concealed or at least not immediately obvious. In the insurance industry, for example, investments were in illiquid securities and real estate, and it took a while before the problems began showing up on balance sheets.

Since mutual funds must buy back their shares on demand, they have to be invested in shares or other securities that are liquid and that can be sold immediately at a known market price. This keeps the fund investing in standard securities and on major markets.

Mutual funds must also value their holdings every day. This is called "marking to market," and it involves tallying all assets and calculating the net asset values. Any problems with a fund's holdings would show up right away in this daily tally.

There are other restrictions involving the investment advisors. They are not allowed to sell their own securities to the fund. This guards against an advisor unloading unsavory stocks and bonds on a fund to the shareholder's detriment. Also, an advisor who is affiliated with a brokerage may not charge excessive commissions.

The Board of Directors

Each fund is organized as a corporation or a trust. The board of directors, its highest authority, is charged with overseeing the management of the fund, the investment objectives, and the manner in which those objectives are carried out by the investment advisors, especially the manager of the portfolio who is the senior investment advisor. The ultimate power of the board is to refuse to renew the contract of the investment advisors, a step rarely taken.

According to law, at least 40 percent of the board of directors must be independent of the management company. This is important because they are charged with watching out for the shareholders' interests, and they can be held personally liable for mismanagement of fund assets.

Although the independent board members are expected to be the shareholders' representatives they are often not known to the shareholders themselves. Their names and principal occupations are reported in the statement of additional information (part B of the prospectus) but few investors ask for that document. Many funds don't even have a shareholders meeting so there is little chance for contact with the independent directors.

HOW IS A FUND ORGANIZED?
▪ ▪ ▪

The **fund** is organized as a corporation or trust with a board of directors.

The **management company** operates the fund on a day-to-day basis. They may be the organizers of the fund.

The **investment advisors** make the decisions as to what securities to buy and sell. They may be the management team or an independent group of security analysts.

The **custodian** keeps the securities but does not enter into investment decisions. Usually this is a bank.

The **transfer agent** records all sales and repurchases of fund shares and keeps shareholder records.

The **distributor** markets the funds to the public or contracts with a brokerage or other marketing team who sells the shares, sends out prospectuses, and contacts prospective customers.

Have There Been Any Cases of Fraud?

In recent years, as a result of SEC investigations, there have been three cases of proven misdeeds. In one case the manager of a group of small mutual funds sold illiquid stock at above-market prices to four of the funds under his advisement. In another case an advisor misstated net asset values and failed to file acceptable reports with the SEC. And in New York and Massachusetts a fund was successfully sued for understating the risk of junk bond funds in their sales pitch and in their prospectus.

However, those suits brought by shareholders against the investment advisors (usually for "breach of fiduciary responsibility") have not fared so well. There has never been a conviction.

WHAT TO DO IF YOU HAVE A PROBLEM
...

If you have a problem with a mutual fund, write to the Securities and Exchange Commission, Room 1065, Stop 10-6, 450 5th Street, N.W., Washington, DC 20549.

THIRTEEN

Taxes

Here's how the IRS views mutual funds: as an intermediary between you and the corporations whose securities the fund holds. The fund itself incurs no taxes, because it makes no profit. All its cash revenues are distributed to its shareholders after the deduction of expenses (management fees, brokerage fees, marketing costs, overhead, etc.). Also, this means that in the eyes of the IRS, mutual funds do not pay dividends, they only pass along cash revenues earned from their portfolios.

All distributions paid to you, the shareholder, are taxable whether you reinvest the distribution or not. How you are taxed depends on the source of the income which the fund reports.

If you received any disbursement from a mutual fund during the calendar year you will receive a Form 1099-DIV. It specifies what was reported to the IRS in the way of disbursements to you. The form contains blanks for four types of payments.

    1a. "Gross dividends and other distributions on stock." This is the amount of all dividend revenue passed through to you by the fund.

    1b. "Ordinary dividends." This will be blank because, as you remember, mutual funds do not pay dividends themselves but only serve as an intermediary funneling the dividends from the securities held by them on to you.

    1c. "Capital gain distribution." All capital gains realized by the fund and distributed to you are shown here.

    1d. "Nontaxable distribution." Depending on the type of fund this may be blank or the largest figure reported.

The form will also state any federal income tax withheld or foreign taxes paid. Capital losses you will not see, but they will have been used to reduce the amount reported on capital gains. Tax laws permit what is called a "tax loss forward" for eight years so that the fund can use net losses in any one year to reduce capital gains for tax purposes in subsequent years.

Taxes and Timing

It was stated earlier that share purchases before or after dividend distributions have no consequences as far as total return, but they *can* have tax consequences. You should plan any major share purchases after an ex-dividend date. Otherwise you could be taxed on the return of your own money. Let us say you made a major share purchase the day before an ex-distribution date. In a couple of weeks you will get a distribution from the fund, and the net asset value of your shares will drop by that exact amount. In effect, you have gotten a portion of your investment back, *but that returned portion is taxable.* No matter that you immediately reinvest it, for IRS purposes that money is a dividend or capital gain: just what your 1099-DIV form will say it is.

Taxes on Sales

When you sell, redeem, or exchange mutual fund shares you incur tax liabilities. Even when you switch funds within the same family of funds, the IRS sees that as the sale of one fund and the purchase of another. The amount of gain or loss is the difference between the amount realized from the sale, exchange or redemption, and what you claim as the cost of the shares. This last point will be explained in the next section.

Which Shares Did You Sell?

For tax purposes, you may want to determine the amount of capital gain or loss any time you sell shares. To do that you must know *which* shares you sold (if you didn't sell all of your shares), and if you have bought shares at different times. You can use one of three methods to determine your capital gain or loss: FIFO (first in first out), or identifiable cost, or by averaging.

With the FIFO method, you assume the shares you are selling are the first ones you bought. This is usually advantageous because it will probably give you the greatest capital gain: The shares would have appreciated over the longest period of time.

If you wished, you could count shares you bought more recently so as to have less capital gain, or perhaps even generate a loss. This is the "identifiable cost" method. You must be certain to carefully identify the shares you sold, and that means going back to your records. (Be *sure* to save all records of purchases). The safest way is to instruct the fund, when you sell, to sell specific shares, giving date of purchase and price, and request confirmation in writing. Submit a copy of your letter and the confirmation with your taxes. Mutual funds send out a Form 1099-B by January 31 which states all your transactions, but this is not a sufficient document on which to base your sale of shares.

The third method is averaging. Much more complicated, it is explained in a booklet from the IRS, number 564.

Don't Tax Yourself Twice

If you are not careful, you could end up paying taxes on some money twice. If your sale involves any shares you might have acquired as reinvestment or by distribution, then you can deduct those shares for the purpose of calculating your capital gains. The point is that the distribution with which you acquired the shares could have shown up on an earlier 1099-DIV form. You've already paid taxes on that money. This is a little complicated and so an illustration is in order.

Let's say that you invested $5,000 last year in a fund and the shares were $10 each (so you bought 500 shares).

Let's say there was one distribution last year of $500 (50 shares) which was reinvested and the shares were still $10. When you sold, the net asset value of the shares had risen to $12. If you sold all 550 shares, the receipt would be $6,600. The amount on which taxes would be owed would not be the difference—$1,600—because you could deduct the $500 used to buy the extra 50 shares. The reason is that you already paid taxes on that amount, which is reported on your last year's 1099-DIV. Only $1,100 of your gain is taxable as capital gain. If you pay taxes on all $1,600, you would be paying taxes on 500 of those dollars twice.

WANT MORE INFORMATION?

• • •

The IRS Publication 564 gives complete instructions as to how to list mutual fund transactions on your income tax. Write to the Internal Revenue Service, U.S. Department of Treasury, 1111 Constitution Avenue, NW, Washington, DC 20274. You can also call the IRS at 800-424-1040. Key in 132 for interest information, 133 for dividend exclusion, 138 for capital gains, 335 for withholding on interest and dividends.

Glossary

Terms of Mutual Funds and the Instruments They Invest In

ADR American Depository Receipt, the form in which foreign securities are usually traded in this country. They are certificates issued by U.S. banks that represent the shares of a foreign corporation held in the country of origin by that bank. A mutual fund that acquires foreign securities through ADRs is acquiring only those foreign securities which trade within this country.

ask or **offering price** The price at which a mutual fund's shares can be purchased. It consists only of the Net Asset Value for no-load funds. For funds with sales charges it is the NAV plus the sales charge or "load," but not a 12b-1 fee, if any.

assets The assets of a mutual fund consist primarily of the securities in its portfolio.

automatic reinvestment A service of mutual funds which permits the investor to designate that all investment dividends and all capital gains distributions be reinvested in the fund.

back-end load *See* load.

bid price The price at which a mutual fund will buy back its shares which is the net asset value. Also called the redemption price.

bond A long-term debt instrument which pays a fixed rate of interest (called the coupon rate) on the face value of the bond (usually $1,000) which is returned to investors at maturity. Interest from bonds issued by state and local agencies is usually tax-exempt. More suitable for income than capital gains, bonds are acquired by some mutual funds depending on the investment objectives of the fund.

break point For some mutual funds, investments beyond a certain amount incur reduced load charges. The amount at which the load charge is reduced is called a break point.

broker A licensed agent who handles security transactions for the public. Shares of mutual funds sold by a broker usually carry a sales charge, called a load.

capital gains Profit made from the sale of securities as opposed to dividends or interest.

capital gains distribution Payment of capital gains to shareholders. Most mutual funds distribute capital gains once a year near the end of the calendar year. For tax purposes capital gains distributions are kept separate from income dividends.

closed-end investment company A company that invests in other companies and has a limited number of shares—like a corporation. It does not buy back its own shares: they trade on the secondary market (on exchanges and over-the-counter) like other common stocks.

contingent deferred sales charge (CDSC) A fee charged investors if they sell their shares within a stated period of time, usually from six months to a few years.

contractual plan An agreement whereby someone agrees to invest a fixed amount of money in a mutual fund on a regular basis for a specified number of years. The fund usually agrees to charge a lower sales fee than would ordinarily apply.

convertible securities Preferred stocks or bonds which have a feature that permits them to be converted into a specified number of common stocks of the issuing company. This becomes profitable when the total market value of the number of shares into which the instrument can be converted exceeds the face value of the convertible stocks or bonds.

coupon rate The fixed rate of interest that a bond pays on its face value, not to be confused with current yield.

current yield The percent of the price paid for mutual fund shares returned annually to the investor in the form of income dividends.

custodian A bank which keeps custody of the securities, cash, and other assets of a mutual fund.

direct marketing A method of selling mutual fund shares whereby investors must call the fund directly to obtain a prospectus and application to purchase shares. The fund usually advertises in newspapers and through the mail, but a sales force, like a brokerage, is not used. This is usually the way no-load funds are marketed.

diversification The spreading of investments among many different securities: a standard method for reducing risk and one of the advantages offered by mutual funds.

dollar-cost averaging The investing of a fixed dollar amount at regular intervals over the long term. Like a contractual plan except that dollar-cost averaging is voluntary and purchases may incur the full sales charge (load).

exchange privilege A service of mutual funds whereby investors may switch their investments from one fund to another within the same family of funds. The number of exchanges per year is usually restricted, and sometimes there is a fee.

face value The amount at which a debt instrument is usually issued and which will be returned to the investor at maturity.

front-end load *See* load.

futures contract An agreement to deliver a stated quantity of a commodity, currency, or financial instrument. Although speculative, they can be used conservatively in order to fine-tune the performance of a portfolio. In the case of stock index futures, the contract is to deliver a group of stocks (or a cash equivalent) that match the contents of a stock index.

Government National Mortgage Association (GNMA) A government corporation that acquires mortgages from banks. Bonds are issued on pools of these mortgages which are in turn often acquired by mutual funds. Interest and principal is passed through to the investor from these bonds.

income dividends Regular payments from mutual funds to their shareholders which are made up of dividends, interest, and short-term capital gains earned from the fund's portfolio. May be distributed annually, bi-annually, quarterly or monthly. Operating expenses of the fund are deducted.

investment advisor The individual, group, or company employed by a mutual fund to provide professional advice on investment and asset management. Includes the portfolio manager who is frequently the founder of the fund.

investment company A company which may be organized as a corporation, partnership, or trust that pools funds to invest in other companies. Mutual funds are an open-end investment company. *See* "closed-end investment company."

investment goals Stated objectives which guide investment programs. Mutual funds are classified on the basis of their investment goals such as growth funds, income funds, tax-free funds, etc.

load A sales charge which, added to the net asset value, makes up the purchase or ask price of those mutual funds known as "load" funds. When the load is charged at the time of purchase it is a front-end load, when charged at redemption it is a back-end load. *See* sales charge.

margin Credit. An amount of cash or securities on deposit as collateral for other securities purchased on credit. Margin increases risk and is only used by some higher-risk funds.

management fee The amount paid to investment advisors of a mutual fund. This fee averages about .5 percent of the fund's assets.

maturity The date on which a bond matures. The face value is returned to the bond holder, and the bond is retired.

municipal bond A debt obligation issued by cities, states, or municipalities the interest from which is exempt from federal tax and some state tax.

mutual fund An open-ended investment company that may sell an unlimited number of shares and that stands ready to buy back those shares at their net asset value. Such a fund offers professional management and broad diversity to investors, large and small. Dividends, interest, and capital gains earned by the fund are passed along to the shareholders after the deduction of expenses.

National Association of Securities Dealers (NASD) An organization of securities brokers and dealers that oversees securities transactions, regulating, among other things, the distribution of mutual fund shares.

NAV *See* net asset value.

net asset value The total market value of a fund's portfolio and other assets, minus expenses, divided by the number of shares outstanding. Always stated as a per-share amount. Calculated at least once daily, this is the price at which the fund will buy back (redeem) its shares from investors. The net asset value always decreases after a dividend payment or capital gains distribution by the amount of the payment or distribution.

open-end investment company A mutual fund.

over-the-counter market (OTC) Securities that do not trade on a securities exchange are said to trade over-the-counter. The OTC market is regulated by the NASD and is made up of an enormous network of securities brokers connected by a computerized trading network.

p-e ratio Price-earnings ratio. One of the measures of the value of stock, it is the number of times the per-share market price of the stock exceeds the per-share earnings. The market price of stock with a high p-e ratio is generally considered to be at greater risk than the market price of stock with a lower p-e ratio. Different industries typically have different average p-e ratios.

preferred stock A type of stock which typically has a large and constant dividend. Technically, it does not constitute equity in the company, as does common stock. Its market price does not fluctuate as much as common stock. Like a bond, it is an instrument that mutual funds acquire for income. Some preferred stock may be converted into the common stock of the issuing company. *See* convertible securities.

prospectus A booklet distributed by a mutual fund which states the fund's investment objectives, all expenses and fees including management and sales fees, a description of shareholder services offered, and information on how to buy shares. Required by the SEC, the fund's prospectus must be in the possession of an investor before he or she can purchase fund shares. A second part of the prospectus, "part B," contains additional information about the fund and is sent on request.

redemption price The price at which mutual funds buy back their shares, usually the net asset value. Also called the bid price.

right of accumulation An agreement whereby an investor can obtain a lower load charge by investing above a specified amount within a specified amount of time.

sales charge The "load" charged on the purchase of mutual fund shares to pay for the sales force marketing the fund's shares. It can be up to 8.5 percent of the amount invested. It is added to the net asset value to determine the ask price of the shares. A "back-end-load" is a sales charge incurred by investors who redeem their shares within a specified time, from six months to several years. *See* load.

Securities and Exchange Commission (SEC) The government agency that regulates the securities industry.

short sale A technique whereby a security is sold that the investor (or fund) does not own. The intention is to buy the security at a later date, after the price has dropped, so as to close out the position. The difference between the two prices is the profit. Conservative mutual funds would not engage in this practice.

single-state funds Municipal tax-free bond funds designed for residents of a particular state.

total performance Usually stated as a percent increase or decrease over the net asset value, this figure takes into consideration all income dividends, capital gains distributions, and the unrealized capital gains of securities still held by the fund.

12b-1 fee An annual fee charged to the fund assets by some mutual funds to pay for the costs of marketing fund shares. It should not exceed 1.25 percent of total fund assets.

warrant A certificate which grants the right to purchase a specified amount of stock in a corporation at a specified price. These certificates, which may be attached to new issues of stock, are traded independently of their underlying stock.

withdrawal plan A service of mutual funds whereby investors may receive regular payments from their funds. The payments may be from dividends and capital gains only or may include principal from the account as needed.

write To sell an option.

yield-to-maturity A measure of the total yield of a bond over its remaining lifetime. It is an annualized percent that takes into consideration the coupon rate (stated percent the bond pays), the current market price of the bond, the capital gain or loss at maturity, and the amount of time until maturity.

If you enjoyed this No Nonsense Guide you may want to order these other No Nonsense Financial Guides: